Walk Worthy. Press On.

Faithful Leaders Grow, Lead, and Finish Well.

Walk Worthy. Press On.
How Faithful Leaders Grow, Lead, and Finish Well

Publisher: Motivate • Lead • Inspire
ISBN: 979-8-9914763-4-8

For bulk orders, speaking engagements, or resources, visit:
www.motivateleadinspire.com

Printed in the United States of America

First Edition

Acknowledgements

No one walks a faithful life alone, and no meaningful work is ever built by one set of hands. This book may have my name on the cover, but it carries the fingerprints of an entire community.

To the friends, family, mentors, leaders, and colleagues who have poured into my faith, my character, and my craft, thank you. Each moment you poured in helped shape not only this book, but the person who wrote it.

There are far too many names to list, and that is one of the greatest blessings of my life.

Thank you to those who challenged me to grow when comfort would have been easier, those who believed in me before I believed in myself, those who spoke truth with love, offered wisdom with humility, and modeled leadership with integrity. And to the quiet encouragers, the behind-the-scenes supporters, and the faithful prayer warriors.

You invested in me long before this book ever existed.

I am especially grateful for the tribe God has surrounded me with, people who live out **hesed**: steadfast love, loyalty, kindness, and covenant faithfulness. Your lives have shown me what it truly means to walk worthy and press on.

This book is, in many ways, a reflection of you.

With deep gratitude and love thank you for walking alongside me.

Walk Worthy. Press On.

There is a quiet assumption many leaders carry, even if we never say it out loud that at some point, we will arrive. That one day we will feel seasoned enough, confident enough, faithful enough to finally say, *I've figured this out* and somehow met all the criteria for leadership excellence.

But the longer I lead and the longer I follow Jesus, the more convinced I am that leadership does not have a finish line. At least not here on this side of eternity.

Scripture never describes leadership as something we master and move beyond. It describes it as something we **walk out.** Step by step, season by season, under the steady, refining hand of God. That is why Paul's words in Ephesians resonate with me:

I therefore, a prisoner for the Lord, urge you to walk in a manner worthy of the calling to which you have been called.
-Ephesians 4:1 (ESV)

Walk. Did you catch that? Not sprint, hustle or arrive. Not achieve the credentials and add the letters after your name. Walk.

Leadership, at its core, is not about reaching a title, having letters after your name, degrees on a wall, or holding a position. It is about how we live out the calling we have already been given. Living out that calling in meetings and conversations, in decisions and conflict, in pressure and perseverance, in faithfulness when no one is watching.

And yet Scripture also holds us in tension. Paul does not only tell us to walk. He tells us to keep going, keep leaning in.

"I press on toward the goal for the prize of the upward call of God in Christ Jesus."
-Philippians 3:14 (ESV)

Leadership requires both walking and pressing on.

- **We are called to walk** worthy with integrity, humility, and alignment to the calling we have received.

  and

- **We are called to press on,** to persevere, to endure, to keep moving forward when leadership gets complex, costly, or unclear.

One without the other eventually breaks us.

Walking without pressing on leads to comfort and stagnation. **Pressing on without walking worthy** leads to burnout, compromise, and drift.

I have spent nearly three decades leading in a wide range of environments; from corporate spaces, teams under pressure, learning and development roles, ministry contexts, seasons of growth, and seasons that required deep recalibration. Along the way, I have taught leadership, coached leaders, built programs, facilitated rooms full of people trying to lead well, and sat quietly with leaders who were exhausted and unsure of their next step.

Alongside that professional experience, I spent over a decade homeschooling my children, years that shaped my understanding of leadership in ways no conference room ever could. I also helped start and lead a nonprofit homeschool co-op for three years, building systems, creating shared culture, aligning families around a common purpose, resolving conflict, developing volunteers, and sustaining a mission that mattered deeply to the people involved.

Those seasons taught me that leadership formation does not happen only in offices or organizations. It happens wherever people are being shaped, supported, and sent forward. It happens in kitchens and classrooms, around folding tables and shared calendars, in moments where vision must be translated into structure and care must be balanced with accountability.

Leadership is learned wherever responsibility meets relationship, and that is holy ground. That's where spiritually grounded, relationally wise, and courageously faithful leaders do His work, in all the places God has already sent them.

Despite all of that experience, perhaps because of it, I can say this with confidence, I am still learning. I am still being formed and corrected. Still discovering where my faith needs to deepen before my leadership can widen.

This book is not written from the finish line. It is written from the road. I am not there, but I am walking alongside you, pressing on with you, and cheering you on as well.

Most believers I know love Jesus deeply. They serve faithfully. They want to honor God with their lives. But they spend forty, fifty, sometimes sixty hours a week leading teams, making decisions, influencing people, shaping culture and no one ever taught them how their faith actually shapes how they lead there.

Leadership training often lives in extremes. It is either overly corporate and disconnected from Scripture, or overly spiritual and disconnected from real life. Very little lives in the middle.

Yet Scripture is full of leadership.

Not just prophets and rabbis, but those historical accounts are filled with administrators, builders, advisors, managers, negotiators, culture shapers, and leaders under pressure. Moses delegated. Nehemiah rebuilt systems. Daniel led with integrity in hostile environments. Esther used influence courageously. Jesus formed people before sending them. Paul developed leaders who would outlast him.

The Bible is already full of leadership frameworks. We simply have not always named them that way.

This book exists to help you see what has been there all along. To help you connect faith and leadership, not as two separate lives you manage, but as one calling you walk out. You don't have to walk it out perfectly or flawlessly. The call is to walk it out faithfully.

Across these pages, we will explore leadership the way Scripture presents it, developmental, formational, relational, and enduring.

We will begin with the inner life before outward influence. We will move through relationships, multiplication, culture, and legacy. Not because leadership is linear, but because formation is intentional.

We will walk through stories, people and verses you may recognize and then discuss frameworks you can use. Each chapter includes questions that slow you down, and practices that shape how you show up tomorrow morning.

This is not about becoming impressive leaders. It is about becoming faithful ones. Leading for an audience of One while impacting your workplace in a way that only you can.

Walking worthy of the calling not once, not frequently, but daily.

Pressing on not in our own strength, but in His.

And we will walk it together because leadership does not end when you get better. It ends when we see Jesus face to face.

Until then, we keep becoming.

Start Here

You Cannot See What You Are Standing In

The Moment

Moses was leading faithfully. From morning until evening, he sat among the people, listening to their disputes and helping them discern what was right. The need was constant. The people were many. And Moses carried the responsibility with seriousness and care. He showed up, he stayed late. He held the weight.

From his perspective, this looked like faithfulness. It looked like obedience to a calling that mattered. But leadership, when lived with that perspective, has a way of normalizing what is slowly becoming unsustainable.

Jethro, Moses' father-in-law, stood outside the daily rhythm and watched. He saw the long lines. He noticed the dependence of the people on one leader. He recognized the quiet assumption that Moses was the only one who could do this work. And then Jethro said what Moses could not see for himself:

"What you are doing is not good" (Exodus 18:17, ESV).

Jethro did not accuse Moses of wrongdoing. He did not question his commitment or diminish the importance of the work. Instead, he named the cost.

"You and the people with you will certainly wear yourselves out," he said. "For the thing is too heavy for you. You are not able to do it alone" (Exodus 18:18, ESV).

And Moses listened. It was almost like Moses heard and reflected and realized that in order to be better at leading, he needed to start leading himself well first. He had to metaphorically look in the mirror, stare at his reflection and start there.

The Leadership Insight

This moment matters because most leadership struggles do not begin with poor intentions. They begin with good ones that are left unexamined.

Moses was not failing as a leader. He was faithful, he cared deeply. He took responsibility seriously. But faithfulness, when paired with unchecked control or unchallenged patterns, can quietly become unsustainable. What Moses needed was not more strength or greater discipline. He needed perspective, someone outside the work who could see what the work was doing to him.

Many leaders find themselves here without realizing it. We confuse being needed with being effective. We confuse responsibility with control. We tell ourselves that if we don't carry it, it won't get done. Over time, leadership becomes heavier, more personal, and more isolating than it was ever meant to be.

This is why this chapter comes first. Before we talk about stages of leadership, before we explore growth or endurance or finishing well, we begin with awareness. Scripture does not simply offer solutions; it invites reflection. And if we do not learn to see ourselves in the story, we will read the rest of this book as wisdom for someone else.

The Leadership Framework

Exodus 18 does not give us a formula to follow. It gives us a pattern to notice.

Leadership that lasts begins with the willingness to pause long enough to see what is actually happening within us and around us. It requires noticing where the work feels heavier than it once did, where leadership has become more isolating, or where responsibility has quietly turned into exhaustion.

From there, **leaders must name what is no longer working**. Not defensively. Not dramatically. Simply honestly. What sustained us in one season may not sustain us in the next.

Only then can we begin to **release what was never meant to be carried alone**. Delegation, in this story, is not abdication. It is stewardship. It creates space for others to grow and allows leadership to multiply rather than bottleneck.

Finally, leadership must be **rebuilt in a way that can endure**. Not through sheer effort, but through shared ownership, trust, and humility. This pattern: notice, name, release, rebuild will surface again throughout this book, not as a checklist, but as a way of seeing leadership clearly.

Leadership in Real Life

Most leaders recognize themselves in Moses more quickly than they expect. It looks like the leader who says yes because no one else will, the leader who feels indispensable and quietly overwhelmed, or the leader who believes letting go will cause things to fall apart. It looks like calendars that are full, decisions that funnel through one person, and a growing sense that leadership has become something to survive rather than sustain.

Often, the problem is not effort, and sometimes the most faithful leadership decision is not to do more, but to lead differently.

Jethro did not replace Moses. He helped him see that leadership was never meant to rest on one set of shoulders. By delegating responsibility and developing others, Moses did not lose influence, he gained longevity. The people were better served. The mission moved forward. And Moses could continue leading without being consumed by the work.

Reflection

As you begin this book, resist the urge to move quickly to solutions.

Instead, consider where leadership currently feels heavier than it should. Notice where you may be holding responsibilities that no longer fit the season you are in. Ask yourself who has permission to speak honestly into your leadership. Ask who can see what you may not be able to see from the inside.

These questions are not meant to discourage you. They are meant to ground you.

Leadership formation begins with truth, not performance.

Where We Begin

Every chapter that follows will invite you into a moment like this, an encounter between Scripture and lived leadership. Each will offer insight, a framework, and a way to carry that wisdom into real life. And as the book unfolds, you will move through different stages of leadership, each building on the last.

But this is where we begin. We begin by looking in the mirror.

Before stages, before strategies, and before forward movement. We start with the person staring back at us, their strengths and limitations, their faithfulness and fatigue, their desire to lead well and their need to grow.

This book is not asking you to fix yourself before you begin. It is asking you to begin with self-awareness. Because leadership that finishes well does not start with answers. It starts with humility and curiosity. With a willingness to see clearly. With openness to wisdom that often comes through others.

We start here *so that* the stories ahead do not remain theoretical. *So that* Scripture becomes a mirror rather than a manual. *So that* as you walk through the stages of leadership, you do so grounded, honest, and ready to be formed.

This is the work beneath the work. And it is where faithful leadership begins.

A Practice for This Week

- Pay attention to where leadership feels most draining right now. Don't rush to fix it. Simply notice it.
- Have one honest conversation with someone you trust. Ask them what they see in how you are leading that you might be missing.
- And release one small responsibility that does not need to rest solely on you. Not to step away from leadership-but to step into it more faithfully.

Stage 1 | Lead Yourself - Character

Inner Formation Before Outer Influence

Every leadership journey begins somewhere, but Scripture is clear about where it begins best. It does not begin with vision statements, titles, credentials, core values on a wall, authority, influence, or strategy. It begins with the heart, with character. With the quiet, unseen work of formation that shapes who we are long before it shapes what we do.

This is where leadership often feels slow, uncomfortable and, let's be real, at times it's awkward. We live in a world that rewards visibility before maturity and results before readiness. Leaders are frequently promoted, praised, or positioned based on skill, personality, or potential, sometimes faster than their inner life can sustain. Momentum builds quickly, but formation lags behind. While outward success can look impressive, Scripture consistently shows that influence without formation eventually collapses under pressure.

That collapse is not a flaw in leadership. It is a warning. Before God expands a leader's reach, He deepens their roots.

Stage 1 is not the most celebrated stage of leadership, but it is the most essential. Everything that follows depends on what is formed here. How you handle pressure. How you speak. How you rest. How you listen. How you respond when obedience costs you something. How you recover when you fall short.

This is a valuable stage where leadership shifts from performance to discipleship. Scripture consistently reveals that God works from the inside out. David was anointed long before he was crowned. Moses was formed in obscurity before confronting Pharaoh. Formation always precedes assignment.

And formation is rarely comfortable. Growth happens in discomfort *so that* something stronger can be built beneath the surface. Character is shaped under tension. Discernment is refined through testing. Integrity is formed through consistency, not convenience.

This is also where many leaders feel the urge to rush ahead. We would rather manage others than examine ourselves. We would rather fix systems than face habits. We would rather learn new strategies than slow down long enough to hear what God might be inviting us to release, reorder, or rebuild.

But Scripture never treats self-leadership as optional. It treats it as foundational.

Jesus Himself modeled this posture. He withdrew to pray. He rested. He resisted temptation. He listened before acting. Even the Son of God did not lead apart from dependence on the Father.

That matters because the way you lead yourself will eventually shape the way you lead everyone else.

- If you do not learn to **abide**, you will burn out.
- If you do not learn to **rest**, you will grasp for control.
- If you do not learn to **guard** your words and the voices you listen to, you will drift.
- If you do not learn to **repent** and receive **grace**, failure will either define you or derail you.

Stage 1 addresses not only how leaders are formed, but how they drift, how they recover, and how they learn to listen again before moving forward.

Throughout this stage, you will encounter themes that may feel countercultural: rest as obedience, conviction without compromise, discernment over noise, integrity in hidden places, grace after failure, and listening as a leadership discipline. These are not soft skills. They are survival skills for leaders who want to remain faithful over time.

This stage is not about becoming a "look at me" leader.

It is about becoming anchored leaders. Leaders who know who they are, who understand their capacity, who can work hard without worshiping busyness.

They are leaders who can hear God's voice even when emotions are loud and circumstances are unclear.

- If you are eager to lead others, start here.
- If you are already leading and feel stretched, distracted, or tired, start here.
- If your leadership looks productive on the outside but feels misaligned on the inside, start here.

Leading yourself is not a detour from leadership. It is the path.

And while it may feel slower than you'd like, it is the only way to build leadership that lasts, leadership rooted in Christ, shaped by character, and sustained by grace.

Let's begin where Scripture always does, looking at the heart of the matter.

Armor of God - Stand Firm Leadership

Resilient leadership under pressure

The Moment

Paul wrote his letter to the Ephesians while under Roman imprisonment, likely chained to a guard. This was not a comfortable season, nor a moment of outward influence or freedom. And yet, from that confined place, Paul offered one of the clearest and most enduring leadership teachings in all of Scripture.

In Ephesians 6:10–18, Paul draws on the imagery directly in front of him, a Roman soldier fully equipped for battle, to describe what it takes to remain faithful under pressure. He does not talk about strategy, advancement, or conquest. He talks about standing. Repeatedly.

"Put on the whole armor of God, that you may be able to **stand** against the schemes of the devil." (Ephesians 6:11, ESV)

"Therefore, take up the whole armor of God, that you may be able to withstand in the evil day, and having done all, to **stand firm**." (Ephesians 6:13, ESV)

This passage is often taught spiritually, and rightly so but it is also profoundly practical for leaders. Paul is speaking to believers navigating resistance, opposition, fatigue, and spiritual attack while remaining faithful to their calling. He is reminding them that leadership endurance is not accidental. It is intentional. It begins with what you put on *before* the pressure comes.

The Leadership Insight

Most leadership failure does not come from a lack of vision or effort. It comes from unprotected inner lives. Leaders rarely fall because they are unskilled. They fall because they are unguarded.

Pressure exposes what formation has (or has not) prepared us for. When resistance shows up, when conflict escalates, when expectations multiply, or when discouragement lingers longer than expected, leadership does not rise to the level of intention. It falls to the level of formation.

Paul reframes leadership strength entirely. Standing firm is not passive. It is not stubbornness or rigidity. It is resilience rooted in truth, character, and spiritual readiness. The armor of God is not about aggression. It is about endurance.

This matters because modern leadership environments, corporate, ministry, education, nonprofit, construction, healthcare, (I could go on, but you get the point) are relentless. Expectations are high. Feedback is constant. Pressure is unending. Leaders are often celebrated for output while quietly falling apart internally.

Paul offers a different leadership metric: *Are you still standing?* Not flashy. Not unshaken. Faithful. Stand-firm leadership is not about avoiding battle. It is about being equipped *so that* when the battle comes, it does not take you out.

The Stand Firm Leadership Framework

Five inner protections every leader needs to sustain pressure without losing integrity.

Truth - The Belt
Truth holds everything together.

Paul begins with the belt of truth because truth stabilizes identity. Leaders drift when they disconnect from what is true about God, about themselves, and about the situation in front of them. Half-truths, self-deception, and unchallenged narratives eventually unravel leadership.

If you lie to yourself, leadership can get unhinged fast. Truth requires honest self-examination, accurate information, and alignment between belief and behavior.

Righteousness - The Breastplate
Righteousness protects the heart.

This is not about perfection. It is about integrity, living in a way that aligns with God's standards even when it costs you something. Leaders who rationalize small compromises eventually normalize bigger ones.

Integrity protects leaders *so that* pressure does not turn into moral erosion. What you excuse privately will surface publicly.

Readiness - The Boots
Paul describes feet fitted with readiness given by the gospel of peace.

Readiness is emotional and spiritual preparedness. It allows leaders to respond instead of react. Unprepared leaders become reactive leaders and reaction rarely produces peace.

Readiness means you have already decided who you are before the moment demands a response.

Faith - The Shield
Faith extinguishes flaming darts like accusation, fear, doubt, and discouragement.

Faith is not denial. It is confidence in God's character when circumstances challenge it. Leaders without faith armor internalize criticism and personalize resistance. Leaders with faith armor discern what to carry and what to drop.

Mindset - The Helmet
The helmet protects the mind, thought patterns, identity, and perspective.

Unprotected minds replay lies as truth and fear as foresight. Mindset determines endurance. Leaders who lose clarity here often quit too early or stay too long in unhealthy patterns.

What This Looks Like at Work

In meetings, **truth** means naming reality clearly. It could be missed KPIs, unmet outcomes, unclear standards, and naming it without blame or spin. Whether you call them KPIs, learning benchmarks, project milestones, job targets, or completion metrics, clarity matters.

In conflict, **righteousness** shows up as integrity under pressure. No gossip, no triangulation, no quiet character erosion to preserve comfort.

In decision-making, **readiness** looks like slowing down *so that* responses are grounded, not reactive. Prepared leaders pause before responding.

In feedback conversations, **faith** helps leaders receive critique without internal collapse or defensive posturing.

Under stress, **mindset protection** prevents catastrophic thinking and burnout spirals.

This framework applies whether you lead a corporate team tracking quarterly results, a ministry navigating volunteer fatigue, a classroom managing learning outcomes, or a construction crew balancing deadlines and safety. Pressure does not change. Formation determines response.

Reflection

- Which piece of armor do you tend to neglect when pressure rises?
- What narratives, true or untrue. most shape how you see yourself as a leader?
- Where might small compromises be quietly weakening your integrity?

If applicable: How does our team protect one another when pressure increases?

Scripture to Read

"Keep your heart with all vigilance, for from it flow the springs of life." -Proverbs 4:23 (ESV)

As you read this verse, what does "guarding your heart" look like in your current leadership season? Where might vigilance and attentiveness be needed right now?

Invite God Into This

Pause for a moment and picture yourself standing, not striving, not proving, just standing.

Ask God to show you where you are protected and where you are exposed. Invite the Holy Spirit to highlight any area where truth needs to be clarified, integrity strengthened, or faith renewed. Pray honestly, not to perform, but to abide.

Leadership pressure is not a sign you are failing. Often, it is evidence you are being trusted with weight. Ask God to help you stand firm, not in your own strength, but in His provision.

Take the Next Step

- **Form a habit:** Begin each workday by intentionally "putting on" one piece of armor in prayer.
- **Have a conversation:** Name truth clearly and graciously in one situation you might normally avoid.
- **Choose a new response:** Eliminate one small compromise that weakens integrity.

Stand firm. not rigidly, but faithfully. Because leadership does not require perfection, it requires formation.

Fruits of the Spirit - Character Core

Maturity before tactics

The Moment

Paul's letter to the Galatians was written into tension. The early church was wrestling with identity, what it meant to live faithfully in Christ without slipping back into rule-keeping on one side or self-indulgence on the other. People were measuring faithfulness by outward behavior, allegiance, and appearance, while missing the deeper work God was doing within them.

In Galatians 5:16–26, Paul redirects their attention. He contrasts life driven by the flesh with life shaped by the Spirit and then offers a simple but profound list. Not of skills to master, but of fruit that grows.

"But the fruit of the Spirit is love, joy, peace, patience, kindness, goodness, faithfulness, gentleness, self-control; against such things there is no law." (Galatians 5:22–23, ESV)

Paul does not present these qualities as goals to achieve. He presents them as evidence. Fruit is not manufactured through effort; it is produced through connection. When the Spirit leads, character follows.

This was not abstract theology. It was pastoral leadership guidance. Paul was reminding believers that maturity shows up less in what we claim to believe and more in how we consistently live.

The Leadership Insight

Most leadership systems reward competence faster than character. We promote people because they are capable, persuasive, productive, or driven. None of those things are inherently wrong. But when competence outpaces character, leadership becomes fragile. It may look impressive, but it lacks staying power.

The fruit of the Spirit offers a different leadership scorecard. These qualities are not soft. They are stabilizing. They determine how leaders respond under pressure, how they treat people when authority is uneven, and how they steward influence when no one is correcting them.

Character is not revealed when things are easy. It is revealed when tension rises, when patience is tested, when joy feels inconvenient, when gentleness requires restraint, and when self-control would be easier to bypass.

This is why fruit matters for leadership.

- Skills get you noticed.
- Character keeps you trusted.

And while tactics can be trained quickly, fruit takes time. It grows through abiding, surrender, obedience, and daily dependence on the Holy Spirit. That process is often uncomfortable. Remember, discomfort is not a sign that something is wrong, it is often a sign something is forming.

Growth happens in discomfort *so that* maturity can develop beneath the surface.

The Character Core Framework

Three leadership-forming movements found in the Fruits of the Spirit.

Relational Fruit - How You Love
Love • Kindness • Goodness

These shape how leaders treat people, especially when power dynamics exist. Love anchors leadership in sacrificial concern for others. Kindness influences tone. Goodness guides ethical decision-making.

Leadership without relational fruit becomes transactional. Results may come, but trust erodes.

Emotional Fruit - How You Carry Pressure

Joy • Peace • Patience

These shape a leader's internal climate. Joy sustains perspective, peace steadies reactions and patience prevents escalation. Leaders set emotional tone whether they intend to or not. What is unsettled or unregulated within a leader eventually affects those around them and it can spread anxiety. Spirit-led leaders cultivate stability.

Disciplinary Fruit - How You Govern Yourself
Faithfulness • Gentleness • Self-Control

These shape consistency over time. Faithfulness builds reliability. Gentleness restrains power. Self-control guards against impulse and overreach.

Talent without self-governance eventually self-destructs. Discipline is not restriction; it is protection *so that* leadership can endure. Together, these nine qualities form a leader's character core, the internal infrastructure that determines how influence is carried.

What This Looks Like at Work

Relational fruit shows up when leaders treat people as people, not resources. In corporate environments, this might look like valuing contribution beyond metrics. In education, it shows up as dignity in discipline. In ministry, it looks like care without favoritism. In trades or construction, it looks like respect on the job site even under deadline pressure.

Emotional fruit shows up when leaders absorb stress instead of amplifying it. Meetings feel calmer. Decisions are clearer. Conflict de-escalates rather than multiplies. Whether you're managing quarterly targets, learning outcomes, production schedules, or volunteer coordination, emotional steadiness becomes contagious.

Disciplinary fruit shows up in consistency. Leaders do what they say they will do. They resist shortcuts. They respond gently instead of harshly. They pause instead of reacting. Over time, this builds credibility that no title can manufacture.

There isn't an easy button for this. Character does not eliminate hard conversations. It determines *how* those conversations are handled.

Reflection

- Which fruit feels most natural for you as a leader? Which feels most strained right now?
- Where might pressure be revealing areas of immaturity rather than failure?
- How does your current leadership environment either support or test your character core?

Scripture to Read

"For God gave us a spirit not of fear but of power and love and self-control."
-2 Timothy 1:7 (ESV)

As you reflect on this verse, which part of your leadership right now most needs love or self-control-not more power or urgency?

Invite God Into This

Take a moment to sit with God-not to fix anything, but to notice.

Ask the Holy Spirit to show you where fruit is growing, even slowly, and where attention may be needed. Invite Him to form character beneath the surface *so that* your leadership can carry greater weight without cracking.

You do not grow fruit by trying harder. You grow fruit by staying connected.

Take the Next Step

- **Form a habit:** At the end of each day, reflect briefly on which fruit was most visible and which was most challenged.
- **Have a conversation:** Name and affirm a fruit you see developing in someone else's leadership.
- **Choose a new response:** Identify one reaction you need to pause before repeating and practice restraint.

Character is not what makes leadership flashy. It is what makes it faithful.

Vine & Branches - Abiding Leadership

Connection before productivity

The Moment

Jesus shared the image of the vine and the branches during one of the most intimate and weighty moments of His ministry. It was the night before His crucifixion. The disciples were unsettled, confused, and anxious about what was coming next. They were about to face uncertainty, loss, and responsibility they felt unprepared to carry.

In John 15:1–17, Jesus does not respond to their anxiety with strategy. He does not give them a plan for growth, expansion, or efficiency. Instead, He gives them a metaphor.

"I am the true vine, and my Father is the vinedresser." (John 15:1, ESV)

And then, over and over again, He repeats the same invitation:

"Abide in me." (John 15:4, ESV)

This teaching comes before their greatest assignment and their greatest testing. Jesus is clear about the order: connection first, fruit later. Abiding is not preparation for leadership; it *is* leadership.

The Leadership Insight

Most leaders are trained to do more when pressure increases. More meetings. More effort. More hours. More urgency.

Jesus teaches the opposite rhythm. In the kingdom of God, fruitfulness does not come from striving harder. It comes from staying connected longer. Leadership effectiveness flows from relationship before responsibility.

This is where leadership has the potential to get a little unhinged. We confuse activity with faithfulness. We assume burnout is a time-management problem instead of a connection problem. We try to solve spiritual depletion with productivity tools.

Jesus offers a radical reframing: *"Apart from me you can do nothing."* (John 15:5, ESV)

Nothing does not mean *little*. It means *nothing that lasts*.

Abiding leadership challenges the lie that value comes from output. It reminds us that leaders are branches, not the vine. We are stewards of influence, not the source of it.

This matters deeply because disconnected leaders eventually over-function. They carry responsibility God never asked them to hold alone. They confuse control with care and exhaustion with faithfulness. Growth happens in discomfort *so that* leaders learn to release what was never theirs to carry.

The Abiding Leadership Framework

Four movements that sustain healthy leadership over time.

Remain - Stay Connected

Abiding begins with presence. To remain is to dwell, to stay close, to make your home in Christ. Leadership does not start with output; it starts with attention.

Leaders who remain connected do not borrow strength from adrenaline or approval. They draw it from relationship.

Receive - Embrace Dependence

Branches do not produce life. They receive it.

This movement confronts the savior complex many leaders quietly carry. Responsibility can masquerade as independence. Control can masquerade as competence.

Receiving reminds leaders that wisdom, strength, clarity, and endurance are gifts, not achievements.

Remove - Accept Pruning

Jesus is clear that even healthy branches are pruned.

Pruning is not punishment. It is preparation. God removes what drains life *so that* fruit can increase. This often feels uncomfortable because it involves letting go. Letting go of good things, familiar rhythms, or roles that once fit but no longer serve.

Leaders resist pruning when identity is tied to busyness.

Reproduce - Bear Fruit
Fruit is the result, not the goal.

You do not tape apples to branches. Fruit grows naturally when connection is healthy. In leadership, fruit shows up as sustained impact, growing others, and influence that multiplies beyond personal effort.

Healthy leaders do not chase results, they cultivate roots.

What This Looks Like at Work

Abiding leadership changes how leaders approach pace. In corporate environments,

Remaining looks like resisting urgency-driven decision-making and building margin before burnout forces it. In education, it looks like presence over performance. In ministry, it looks like serving without saviorism and heroics. In trades and operations, it looks like safety, consistency, and focus over speed alone.

Receiving shows up when leaders ask for help sooner, delegate earlier, and admit uncertainty without fear. Whether you call it workload distribution, team development, or shared accountability, dependence strengthens systems.

Pruning shows up when leaders stop doing work that no longer aligns with calling or impact. It might mean fewer initiatives, clearer priorities, or boundaries around availability. Pruning always feels risky but unpruned growth eventually collapses under its own weight.

Fruit shows up over time. Teams become healthier. Turnover decreases. Trust increases. Outcomes stabilize. The work feels less frantic and more faithful.

Abiding does not make leadership passive, it makes it sustainable.

Reflection

- Where are you currently striving when Jesus may be inviting you to remain?
- What responsibilities might you be carrying that God never asked you to own alone?
- What would pruning look like in this season, not as loss, but as alignment?

Scripture to Read

“Abide in me, and I in you. As the branch cannot bear fruit by itself, unless it abides in the vine, neither can you, unless you abide in me.”
-John 15:4 (ESV)

As you read this verse, what does abiding look like practically in your current leadership rhythm?

Invite God Into This

Slow your breathing for a moment. Ask God to reveal where connection has been replaced by striving. Invite Him to show you what needs to remain, what needs to be received, and what may need to be removed.

You do not need to force fruit, you are invited to stay connected.

Take the Next Step

- **Form a habit:** Begin or end each workday with a brief moment of intentional connection with God before engaging tasks.
- **Have a conversation:** Name one boundary or support you need in order to lead more sustainably.
- **Choose a new response:** Create a "stop-doing" list and remove one low-impact activity.

Abiding is not a retreat from leadership. It is the root of it.

Daniel - Conviction Without Compromise

Integrity in hostile environments

The Moment

Daniel's leadership story begins in disruption. As a young man, Daniel was taken from Jerusalem and placed into the heart of Babylon's empire, a foreign, powerful, and openly hostile system.

Everything familiar was stripped away: language, culture, rhythms, and even his name. He was trained to serve a government that did not share his values and rewarded conformity over conviction.

Daniel 1 tells us that while Daniel was enrolled in the king's training program, he made a quiet but decisive choice:

"Daniel resolved that he would not defile himself with the king's food, or with the wine that he drank." (Daniel 1:8, ESV)

This was not rebellion. It was resolve.

Later, in Daniel 6, that same conviction reappears under far greater pressure. Daniel's faithfulness made him stand out and is integrity made him a target. When a law was passed that directly conflicted with his devotion to God, Daniel did not panic, posture, or perform.

"When Daniel knew that the document had been signed, he went to his house... and got down on his knees three times a day and prayed and gave thanks before his God, as he had done previously." (Daniel 6:10, ESV)

No speeches. No outrage. No drama. Just consistency. Daniel did not *become* faithful under pressure. He *revealed* what had already been formed.

The Leadership Insight

Most leaders don't lose integrity all at once. They lose it slowly through small accommodations, quiet rationalizations, and unexamined compromises made in the name of survival, success, or being "realistic."

Daniel shows us a different path. Conviction is not loud. Integrity is not reactive. Faithfulness is not situational. Daniel's leadership was effective *because* his convictions were settled long before the pressure arrived. He did not wait until the lion's den to decide what he believed. He decided long before that moment, in private.

This matters deeply for modern leaders because many of us operate inside systems that do not reward conviction. Corporate environments, ministries, educational institutions, nonprofits, and government organizations all have unspoken rules around what gets praised, what gets overlooked, what is quietly expected. The danger is not opposition. The danger is normalization.

When leaders normalize compromise, integrity becomes optional. When integrity becomes optional, leadership becomes unstable. Daniel reminds us that conviction is not about defiance. It is about alignment. And alignment always costs something.

The Conviction Without Compromise Framework

Four practices that anchor leaders in integrity within hostile or misaligned systems.

Decide Early - Set Convictions Before Pressure
Daniel "resolved" in advance. Conviction formed ahead of conflict removes decision fatigue later. Leaders who wait to decide under pressure often decide poorly. Pre-deciding values creates stability when stakes rise.

Respect Authority - Without Surrendering Integrity
Daniel did not demean leadership or posture against authority. He remained respectful while remaining faithful. Healthy conviction does not require hostility. It requires clarity.

Practice Consistency - Private Before Public
Daniel's habits did not change when scrutiny increased. His private rhythms sustained public faithfulness. Integrity is built in repetition, not reaction.

Trust God With Outcomes - Release Control
Daniel obeyed without knowing the result. Conviction does not guarantee safety, it guarantees faithfulness.

Leaders often compromise because they fear consequences more than misalignment. Daniel trusted God with what he could not control.

What This Looks Like at Work

In modern workplaces, conviction shows up when leaders refuse to manipulate data, inflate outcomes, or misrepresent reality, whether those numbers are KPIs, learning metrics, production targets, or safety reports.

In education or ministry, conviction shows up when leaders resist favoritism, performative spirituality, or pressure to prioritize optics over formation.

In operations, construction, or trades, conviction shows up when leaders choose safety, honesty, and respect even when deadlines push back.

Conviction without compromise does not make leadership easier. It makes it trustworthy. And trust compounds.

Reflection

- Where are you currently feeling pressure to quietly conform rather than stand aligned?
- Which convictions have you clearly decided-and which have you left vague?
- What daily habits either strengthen or erode your integrity?

Scripture to Read

"But Daniel resolved that he would not defile himself..."
-Daniel 1:8 (ESV)

As you reflect on this verse, what is one area where you need to resolve *before* pressure increases?

Invite God Into This

Ask God to show you where conviction needs clarity, not for performance, but for alignment.

Invite the Holy Spirit to strengthen your resolve *so that* obedience does not depend on circumstance or approval.

Pray for the courage to be consistent, not dramatic.

Take the Next Step

- **Form a habit:** Identify one non-negotiable value and write it down clearly.
- **Have a conversation:** Name a boundary respectfully where expectations feel misaligned.
- **Choose a new response:** Reinforce a private habit that supports public integrity.

Sabbath - Rest Is Obedience

Capacity, rhythm, and faithful work

The Moment

The concept of Sabbath appears before leadership roles, before nations, before systems, and before sin enters the story.

In Genesis 2, after creating the world, God rests.

“And on the seventh day God finished his work that he had done, and he rested on the seventh day from all his work that he had done.” (Genesis 2:2, ESV)

God did not rest because He was tired. He rested because He was finished. Rest was not recovery, it was completion. Boundary. Declaration.

Later, when God gives the Ten Commandments, Sabbath is not offered as a suggestion or a reward for good behavior. It is commanded.

“Remember the Sabbath day, to keep it holy.” (Exodus 20:8, ESV)

Sabbath is framed as obedience, not indulgence. It is woven into God's design for human flourishing, not as an escape from work, but as a rhythm that makes work faithful and sustainable.

Jesus reinforces this rhythm when He says,

"The Sabbath was made for man, not man for the Sabbath." (Mark 2:27, ESV)

Sabbath is not restriction. It is provision.

The Leadership Insight

Modern leadership culture tends to swing between two unhealthy extremes.

On one side is **hustle culture**-the belief that busyness equals faithfulness, exhaustion equals importance, and rest is a reward for later. This mindset relabels overwork as virtue and quietly teaches leaders that slowing down is weakness.

On the other side is a gentler but equally incomplete reaction what many now call the **soft life culture**. It's the posture that prioritizes comfort and ease to the point of disengagement, treating work as merely transactional and disconnecting effort from purpose. The pendulum swings from over-functioning to under-engaging.

Both extremes miss the biblical vision of work.

Scripture does not call us to grind ourselves into the ground, nor does it invite us to disengage from responsibility. It calls us to **faithful work**.

"Whatever you do, work heartily, as for the Lord and not for men." (Colossians 3:23, ESV)

We work diligently *because* we are working for God and we rest faithfully *because* we trust God.

Sabbath confronts the lie that busy equals successful *and* the lie that minimal effort equals freedom. It invites leaders into a third way, a rhythm that honors capacity, purpose, and trust.

This is where leadership gets uncomfortable because Sabbath forces leaders to acknowledge limits. It exposes control and reveals whether our identity is rooted in calling or performance.

Growth happens in this discomfort *so that* leaders learn to lead from obedience rather than adrenaline.

The Faithful Rhythm Framework

Honor both work and rest without falling into either extreme.

Work Wholeheartedly - Engage with Integrity
Biblical rest does not diminish effort. Leaders are called to work with excellence, diligence, and responsibility. Half-hearted leadership dishonors both people and purpose.

Faithful leaders bring their full selves to the work God has given them, whether that work is leading teams, teaching students, serving clients, building structures, or caring for people.

Stop Intentionally - Practice Obedience
Sabbath requires stopping *on purpose*. Not collapsing from exhaustion. Not disengaging out of resentment. Choosing to stop as an act of trust.

Stopping says, “I am not the source. God is.”

Trust Provision - Release Control
Rest reveals where leaders rely on effort instead of God. When leaders stop, they confront the fear that things will fall apart without them.

Sabbath answers that fear with trust.

Return Renewed - Lead from Capacity
Sabbath is not withdrawal from leadership. It is preparation for it. Rested leaders return with clarity, patience, and discernment. They lead from capacity instead of depletion.

This rhythm does not eliminate pressure. It makes leadership resilient.

What This Looks Like at Work

In corporate environments, faithful rhythm looks like setting boundaries around availability, resisting performative busyness, and modeling sustainable pace while still owning outcomes, goals, and responsibilities.

In education and ministry, it looks like caring deeply without becoming indispensable, serving faithfully without martyrdom, and honoring rest without guilt.

In trades, operations, or high-demand roles, it looks like valuing safety, consistency, and recovery as part of excellence, not obstacles to productivity.

Sabbath reframes leadership success. It asks not just *what* was accomplished, but *how* it was carried.

- **Leaders who never rest** eventually lead from irritation, tunnel vision, or burnout.
- **Leaders who disengage** lose influence and trust.
- **Leaders who honor rhythm** lead with steadiness and credibility.

Reflection

- Where do you most feel the pull toward hustle or toward disengagement?
- How do you personally define success, and who shaped that definition?
- What signals tell you that you are operating beyond healthy capacity?

Scripture to Read

"It is in vain that you rise up early and go late to rest, eating the bread of anxious toil; for he gives to his beloved sleep."
-Psalm 127:2 (ESV)

As you reflect on this verse, where might anxious toil be replacing trust in your leadership right now?

Invite God Into This

Take a breath and sit with God honestly.

Ask Him to reveal where your rhythm reflects trust and where it reflects fear. Invite Him to help you see rest not as escape, but as obedience. Ask for wisdom to work hard *and* rest well, without shame, without striving, and without disengagement.

Let God redefine what faithfulness looks like in this season.

Take the Next Step

- **Form a habit:** Choose one consistent time to stop working and honor rest without justification.
- **Have a conversation:** Clarify expectations or boundaries that protect healthy rhythm.
- **Choose a new response:** Replace one habit of anxious busyness with intentional trust.

Sabbath does not make leaders less effective, it makes them faithful.

Words & Voices - What We Speak, Hear, and Believe

Language shapes leadership

The Moment

Scripture is remarkably consistent about one thing: words are never neutral.

From the beginning, creation itself unfolds through speech. God speaks, and worlds form. Light appears. Order emerges. Life takes shape. Words initiate reality.

And then, in Genesis 3, we see the first fracture, not through force, but through conversation.

The serpent does not attack Eve. He questions her by asking,

"Did God actually say...?" (Genesis 3:1, ESV)

With a single sentence, a competing voice enters the story. God's words are not denied outright, they were reframed, softened, distorted. What follows is not just disobedience, but confusion about who to trust, what to believe, and which voice should hold authority.

Centuries later, James echoes this same truth in a very different context:

"The tongue is a small member, yet it boasts of great things." (James 3:5, ESV)

James is writing to believers navigating conflict, comparison, and community strain. His warning is blunt. Words direct lives the way a rudder directs a ship. Small, seemingly insignificant statements can set entire systems on fire.

From Eden to the early church, Scripture draws a straight line: What we say, what we hear, and what we believe determine our direction.

The Leadership Insight

Leadership lives or dies by language. I know it may sound extreme, but I challenge you to hear me out. Not just formal communication, but emails, texts, Slack, Teams, meetings, feedback, leadership shows up in the words leaders repeat internally and externally. The stories they tell. The assumptions they reinforce. The voices they allow to shape their decisions.

Most leadership derailment does not begin with action. It begins with unchecked narratives. It could be a quiet voice says, You're falling behind. Another says, This is just how it's done here. Another whispers, If you don't control this, everything will fall apart.

Left unexamined and unchecked, these voices gain authority.

James warns that leaders who cannot govern their speech cannot govern much else. And Genesis reminds us that discernment failure rarely sounds evil, it sounds reasonable.

This is where leadership can get unhinged. We assume maturity automatically filters voices. It doesn't. Discernment must be practiced. Leaders must learn to filter what they hear, steward what they say, and examine what they believe, especially under pressure.

Words shape culture *so that* beliefs take root and behaviors follow.

The Words & Voices Framework

Four leadership disciplines that protect direction and integrity.

Notice the Source - Who Is Speaking?
Every voice has an origin. God's voice leads with truth and clarity. Competing voices often lead with doubt, fear, urgency, or comparison.

Leaders must learn to ask, *Where is this narrative coming from?* Not every internal thought deserves authority.

Test the Message - Is It True?
Eve did not test the serpent's words against what God had actually said. Leaders often do the same, accepting assumptions, industry norms, or emotional reactions as truth.

Truth tested early prevents correction later.

Guard the Mouth - What Am I Releasing?
James makes this unavoidable: leaders set tone with their words. Sarcasm, cynicism, exaggeration, and careless comments shape environments faster than policy ever will.

What leaders tolerate verbally, culture absorbs relationally.

Examine the Belief - What Has Taken Root?
Words repeated become beliefs. Beliefs shape decisions. Decisions shape outcomes.

Leaders must regularly ask, What do I believe about myself, my people, and God right now, and who taught me that?

Unexamined beliefs quietly steer leadership off course.

What This Looks Like at Work

In meetings, this shows up in how leaders frame challenges. Words like *always*, *never*, *they*, and *can't* create limitation cultures. Words like *learn*, *clarify*, and *adjust* create growth cultures.

In feedback, it shows up in whether leaders speak truth with care or weaponize honesty without wisdom. In emails, it shows up in tone. In conflict, it shows up in whether leaders escalate fear or invite clarity.

Internally, it shows up in the narratives leaders repeat when decisions are hard, whether those narratives are rooted in trust or control.

Whether you lead in corporate environments, classrooms, ministry teams, or trades, language determines climate. You may call it communication, culture, morale, or engagement, but Scripture calls it stewardship.

Reflection

- Which voices most influence your leadership decisions right now?
- Where might you be accepting narratives without testing them against truth?
- How does your language (spoken or internal) shape the culture around you?

Scripture to Read

"Let the words of my mouth and the meditation of my heart be acceptable in your sight, O LORD."
-Psalm 19:14 (ESV)

As you read this verse, what connection do you notice between your inner dialogue and your outward leadership?

Invite God Into This

Ask God to tune your ear to His voice above all others.

Invite the Holy Spirit to surface any beliefs that have formed from fear, pressure, or comparison rather than truth. Pray for restraint in speech, clarity in discernment, and humility to be corrected when needed.

Ask God to align what you say, hear, and believe *so that* your leadership reflects His heart.

Take the Next Step

- **Form a habit:** Pause before responding in moments of tension and ask, What voice am I responding from?
- **Have a conversation:** Clarify or correct a narrative that may be shaping your team unfairly.
- **Choose a new response:** Replace one recurring negative or anxious phrase with language grounded in truth.

Words create worlds and wise leaders steward them carefully.

David & Bathsheba - Hidden Compromise

What leaders excuse in private eventually surfaces in public

The Moment

David's failure does not begin with Bathsheba. That's the part we often rush past. Second Samuel 11 opens with a detail that feels almost incidental, but it is anything but:

"In the spring of the year, the time when kings go out to battle, David sent Joab... But David remained at Jerusalem." (2 Samuel 11:1, ESV)

David was not where he was supposed to be. The king stayed home while others went to war. There is no explanation offered, no justification. Just absence. A subtle deviation from rhythm and responsibility.

What follows is tragically familiar. David sees what he should not have lingered on. He asks questions he should not have pursued. He takes what was not his. And when consequences begin to surface, he shifts from desire to deception, from concealment to calculation.

The collapse is not immediate. It is progressive. Sin multiplies. Lies compound. A faithful man, Uriah, is betrayed and killed. And David, the anointed king, attempts to manage the fallout rather than confront the truth.

It is only when the prophet Nathan speaks through story, not accusation, that David finally sees himself clearly.

"You are the man." (2 Samuel 12:7, ESV)

And with that moment of clarity, the illusion shatters.

The Leadership Insight

Most leadership failure is not explosive. It is incremental.

Leaders rarely wake up intending to compromise their integrity. They drift there through fatigue, entitlement, isolation, and unchecked desire. Through moments where no one seems to be watching. Through small permissions granted quietly.

David did not fall because he lacked gifting. He fell because he stopped guarding his inner life.

This is the danger of hidden compromise.

What leaders excuse privately eventually shows up publicly. Not always immediately. Sometimes years later. Sometimes through unintended consequences rather than direct exposure.

The tension here is uncomfortable because many leaders resonate with David not in action, but in pattern. Staying disengaged longer than intended. Letting discipline slide. Allowing boredom, success, or exhaustion to dull discernment.

Scripture does not include this story to shame leaders. It includes it to warn them.

Leadership does not fail in moments of weakness alone. It fails when weakness goes unexamined.

The Hidden Compromise Framework

Four warning signs leaders must take seriously.

Idle Disengagement - Stepping Away from Rhythm
David was idle when he should have been engaged. Leadership rhythm matters. When leaders disengage from responsibility without intention, vulnerability increases.

Idle time is not rest. It is unguarded space.

Private Permission - Allowing What Should Be Refused
Compromise rarely feels dramatic. It feels justified. Private permission creates private patterns that eventually demand public consequence.

Covering Behavior - Managing Image Instead of Truth
When leaders shift from confession to concealment, the cost multiplies. Protecting image becomes more important than restoring integrity.

Confronted Clarity - Facing Reality Honestly
Nathan's courage exposes David's blindness. Leadership requires voices that tell the truth even when it hurts.

Restoration begins where denial ends.

What This Looks Like at Work

In modern leadership contexts, hidden compromise rarely looks like scandal at first. It looks like misrepresenting progress. Overlooking policy violations. Justifying harshness. Ignoring burnout. Letting boundaries erode "just this once."

In corporate settings, it might involve manipulating data or shifting blame. In ministry or education, it might involve moral shortcuts disguised as calling. In operations or trades, it might involve cutting corners under pressure.

Compromise thrives in isolation. Healthy leadership invites accountability.

Leaders do not need perfection. They need vigilance.

Reflection

- Where might you be disengaged from rhythms that once protected you?
- What small permissions have you normalized that deserve reexamination?
- Who has the right to speak truth into your leadership right now?

Scripture to Read

"Search me, O God, and know my heart! Try me and know my thoughts!"
-Psalm 139:23 (ESV)

As you sit with this verse, what might God be inviting you to bring into the light?

Invite God Into This

Come to God without defensiveness.

Ask Him to reveal anything hidden, not to condemn, but to heal. Invite the Holy Spirit to restore clarity, humility, and courage. Pray for a heart that responds quickly to conviction rather than slowly through consequence.

God does not expose to destroy. He exposes to restore.

Take the Next Step

- **Form a habit:** Recommit to one rhythm that keeps you spiritually and emotionally anchored.
- **Have a conversation:** Invite honest feedback from someone you trust.
- **Choose a new response:** Interrupt one pattern that thrives in secrecy.

Hidden compromise never stays hidden, but repentance always opens the door to renewal.

Peter’s Restoration - Failure Isn’t Final

Grace that rebuilds leadership

The Moment

Peter’s failure was not subtle. He did not drift quietly or compromise slowly. He denied Jesus publicly, repeatedly, and emphatically at the very moment loyalty mattered most.

Just hours earlier, Peter had declared unwavering devotion.

“Even if I must die with you, I will not deny you.” (Matthew 26:35, ESV)

And yet, when pressure rose and fear took hold, Peter collapsed under the weight of his own confidence.

“Then he began to invoke a curse on himself and to swear, ‘I do not know the man.’” (Matthew 26:74, ESV)

Luke tells us that in that moment, Jesus turned and looked at Peter.

“And Peter remembered the saying of the Lord... And he went out and wept bitterly.” (Luke 22:61–62, ESV)

The denial is devastating. But it is not the end of Peter's story.

After the resurrection, Jesus does not confront Peter publicly. He does not disqualify him quietly. He does not sideline him permanently. Instead, in John 21, Jesus meets Peter on the shore over breakfast, not a dark alley or courtroom. There, Jesus asks Peter the same question three times:

"Do you love me?" (John 21:15–17, ESV)

For every denial, an invitation. For every failure, a restoration.

The Leadership Insight

Many leaders believe failure is fatal. Not officially, few would say that out loud, but functionally. They assume that once credibility is damaged, leadership is over. That mistakes permanently define capacity. That grace is for salvation, but leadership requires perfection.

Peter's story dismantles that lie. Failure does not disqualify leaders. Unrepented failure does.

Jesus does not ignore Peter's failure. He addresses it directly. He does not rehearse it endlessly either. He restores Peter through relationship, responsibility, and recommissioning.

This matters because leaders often respond to failure in one of two unhealthy ways: shame or avoidance.

Shame convinces leaders they are finished.

Avoidance convinces them nothing needs to change.

Jesus chooses neither. He restores honestly and purposefully. Growth happens in this tension *so that* leaders are formed by grace rather than crushed by guilt.

The Restoration Leadership Framework

Four steps to restoration after failure.

Name It - Acknowledge What Happened
Jesus does not pretend Peter's denial didn't occur. Restoration begins with truth, not defensiveness.

Leaders who name failure clearly create space for healing. Leaders who avoid it remain stuck.

Receive Grace - Accept What Is Offered
Jesus does not demand penance. He offers presence. Grace must be received, not earned.

Many leaders struggle here, believing they must punish themselves longer than God requires.

Recommit - Say Yes Again
Jesus asks Peter if he loves Him, not if he regrets his actions. Love re-anchors calling.

Leadership recommits to relationship before responsibility.

Return to Responsibility - Serve with Humility
"Feed my sheep" is not a consolation prize. It is restored assignment.

Restored leaders lead differently. The are less self-reliant, more compassionate, more grounded.

What This Looks Like at Work

In leadership contexts, failure may look like a poor decision, a relational rupture, a missed ethical moment, or a season of burnout that impacted others. Whether the failure is public or private, leaders must decide what story they will tell themselves next.

Healthy restoration includes acknowledgment, ownership, and changed behavior. It does not require self-erasure.

In corporate environments, this might look like rebuilding trust through consistency. In ministry or education, it may involve stepping back briefly before stepping forward wisely. In operations or trades, it may involve retraining, recalibration, or recommitment to standards.

Restored leaders do not lead from ego. They lead from gratitude.

Reflection

- How do you typically respond to failure? Shame, defensiveness, avoidance, or humility?
- What failure are you still letting define your leadership identity?
- Where might Jesus be inviting you to recommit rather than withdraw?

Scripture to Read

"The LORD is near to the brokenhearted and saves the crushed in spirit." -Psalm 34:18 (ESV)

As you reflect on this verse, what would it look like to lead from grace rather than guilt?

Invite God Into This

Bring your failure to God without minimizing or magnifying it.

Ask Him to help you see it clearly, not as a final verdict, but as a place where grace can do its deepest work. Invite Jesus to restore what fear, pride, or exhaustion damaged.

Let grace shape your next step, not shame.

Take the Next Step

- **Form a habit:** When you notice self-criticism after a mistake, replace it with truthful grace.
- **Have a conversation:** Acknowledge a misstep honestly with someone it affected.
- **Choose a new response:** Adjust one pattern that contributed to the failure.

Failure is not the end of leadership. Grace gets the final word.

Elijah & the Whisper - Listen Before You Act

Discernment in exhaustion and transition

The Moment

Elijah's story reaches its emotional peak in 1 Kings 18. He confronts false prophets. He calls down fire from heaven. He leads a national reckoning. It is one of the most dramatic displays of God's power in Scripture and Elijah is at the center of it.

And then, almost immediately, everything unravels.

In 1 Kings 19, Elijah receives a threat from Jezebel, panics, and runs. The prophet who stood unshaken before crowds collapses in isolation. He flees into the wilderness, exhausted and afraid, and prays a startling prayer:

"It is enough; now, O LORD, take away my life." (1 Kings 19:4, ESV)

This is not rebellion. It is burnout. God does not correct Elijah first. He does not lecture him, He lets Elijah sleep. He feeds him, He restores his physical strength before addressing his spiritual confusion.

Then God invites Elijah to Mount Horeb not to relive the fire, but to relearn how to listen. There is a great wind. An earthquake. A fire. But God is not in any of them.

"And after the fire the sound of a low whisper." (1 Kings 19:12, ESV)

And Elijah listens.

The Leadership Insight

Many leaders assume that clarity comes through intensity. More urgency. More pressure. More noise.

But Scripture repeatedly shows the opposite. God often speaks most clearly after the noise subsides, when leaders are still enough to hear Him.

Elijah's collapse was not due to lack of faith or courage. It was the result of prolonged output without recalibration. He had poured himself out faithfully and had nothing left to draw from.

This is where leadership gets quietly dangerous. When leaders are exhausted, discernment weakens. Fear grows louder. Perspective narrows. Decisions become reactive instead of reflective. Leaders mistake urgency for instruction.

God meets Elijah not in the spectacular, but in the subtle. Not in the adrenaline, but in the whisper.

Growth happens here *so that* leaders learn to discern God's voice even when emotions are loud and energy is low.

The Listening Leadership Framework

How leaders learn to listen well, especially in seasons of fatigue or transition.

Acknowledge Exhaustion - Name What's True
Elijah admits he is done. God meets him there.

Leaders must name exhaustion honestly before they can hear clearly. Ignoring fatigue does not make leaders strong; it makes them reactive.

Restore Capacity - Tend to the Body
God addresses Elijah's physical needs before his calling. Rest and nourishment are not spiritual distractions, they are prerequisites for discernment.

Faithful leaders respect embodiment.

Create Quiet - Step Away from Noise
God invites Elijah out of chaos and into stillness. Discernment requires space.

Leaders must intentionally step away from constant input, opinions, alerts, urgency *so that* God's voice can be distinguished.

Listen and Respond - Move with Clarity
God's whisper does not end Elijah's calling. It redirects it. Elijah receives new assignments, new perspective, and the knowledge that he is not alone.

Listening leads to next steps not panic.

What This Looks Like at Work

In leadership roles today, noise is constant. Meetings, messages, metrics, crises, opinions, and expectations compete for attention. Leaders are praised for speed, not stillness.

Listening leadership looks like slowing decisions long enough to discern wisdom. It looks like resisting pressure to react immediately. It looks like building margin into leadership rhythms.

In corporate settings, this might mean pausing before restructuring or responding to conflict. In education or ministry, it may mean discerning calling rather than defaulting to obligation. In trades or operations, it may mean prioritizing safety and clarity over urgency.

Leaders who listen well do not lead less. They lead *better*.

Reflection

- Where might exhaustion be shaping your leadership more than discernment?
- What "noise" most interferes with your ability to hear God clearly?
- When was the last time you intentionally paused before making a decision?

Scripture to Read

"Be still, and know that I am God."
-Psalm 46:10 (ESV)

As you sit with this verse, what would stillness look like in your current leadership season?

Invite God Into This

Sit quietly with God.

Resist the urge to fill the space with words. Ask Him to help you recognize His voice, not just in dramatic moments, but in gentle nudges, quiet convictions, and steady clarity.

Invite Him to restore your capacity and guide your next steps.

Listening is not passive. It is an act of trust.

Take the Next Step

- **Form a habit:** Build one intentional pause into your week where no input is allowed.
- **Have a conversation:** Ask for perspective rather than validation.
- **Choose a new response:** Delay one decision until you've created space to listen.

God does not only speak in fire. Often, He whispers. And wise leaders learn to listen.

Stage 2 | Lead a Team - Relationships

How You Show Up to People

If **Stage 1** is about who you are becoming, **Stage 2** is about how that formation shows up in real relationships.

Leadership does not stay internal for long. Eventually, it moves outward into conversations, meetings, conflict, collaboration, encouragement, correction, and care. The way you lead yourself will always surface in how you lead others, whether you intend it to or not.

This is where leadership becomes visible.

You can often tell how much inner work a leader has done by how people feel around them. Are others at ease or on edge? Do they feel seen or managed? Are mistakes handled with dignity or defensiveness? Is trust growing or quietly eroding?

Scripture is unambiguous here: how we treat people reveals what we truly believe about God, authority, and responsibility.

Stage 2 shifts the focus from internal formation to relational impact. It asks not just *What kind of leader am I becoming?* but *What kind of environment am I creating for others?*

This is where leadership gets personal.

Relationships expose gaps that private disciplines can hide. You can pray faithfully and still speak carelessly. You can rest well and still avoid hard conversations. You can hold strong convictions and still misuse authority. **Stage 2** brings those tensions into the open-not to shame leaders, but to mature them.

Jesus consistently modeled this progression. He did not simply teach truth; He lived it among people. He noticed the overlooked. He served in ways that disrupted hierarchy. He encouraged growth before demanding performance, spoke truth directly, but never carelessly. He built rhythms that sustained community, not just moments that inspired it.

This stage will challenge how you:

- Show up in everyday interactions,
- Respond to need and interruption,
- Use your words and tone,
- Give feedback and correction,
- Share responsibility,
- Build trust over time.

The goal is not relational perfection. It is relational faithfulness.

Healthy teams are not built through charisma, control, or constant harmony. They are built through presence, consistency, courage, and care applied over time, in ordinary moments.

As you move through this stage, you may notice patterns in your leadership that feel familiar. You may also notice discomfort. That is not failure. That is formation continuing its work.

Growth still happens in discomfort only now, it happens in community.

Stage 2 will invite you to lead closer to people, not above them. To see relationships not as obstacles to productivity, but as the primary place where leadership is lived out. To recognize that culture is shaped less by policies and more by everyday interactions.

If **Stage 1** asked you to slow down and listen, **Stage 2** will ask you to step in and engage wisely, humbly, and intentionally.

Because leadership is never just about what you do. It is about how people experience you while you are doing it.

Let's keep going.

Washing Feet - Servant Presence Leadership

Authority expressed through service

The Moment

John 13 takes place on the night Jesus knows everything is about to change. The disciples are gathered for Passover. Tension is already in the room. Questions are unspoken. Power dynamics are present, even if no one names them. They are still debating status, influence, and who matters most among them.

And Jesus does something no one expects.

"Jesus, knowing that the Father had given all things into his hands, and that he had come from God and was going back to God, rose from supper." (John 13:3–4, ESV)

That line matters. Jesus acts *from* authority, not toward it.

He takes off His outer garment, wraps a towel around His waist, pours water into a basin, and begins to wash the disciples' feet. This is not symbolic abstraction. It is physical, awkward, intimate work. Work normally reserved for the lowest servant in the household.

Peter protests - of course he does.

"You shall never wash my feet." (John 13:8, ESV)

The discomfort is real. Servant leadership sounds inspiring until it requires proximity. Until it disrupts hierarchy and feels beneath us.

When Jesus finishes, He does not leave the moment open-ended.

"You call me Teacher and Lord, and you are right, for so I am. If I then, your Lord and Teacher, have washed your feet, you also ought to wash one another's feet." (John 13:13–14, ESV)

This is not a personality preference, it is a leadership directive.

The Leadership Insight

Servant leadership is often misunderstood as softness, passivity, or lack of authority. Jesus dismantles that misunderstanding completely.

He washes feet *because* He knows who He is. He does not serve to earn authority. He serves from authority. His identity is settled, so His posture is free. This distinction matters deeply for leaders.

- **Insecure leaders** use power to protect themselves.
- **Secure leaders** use power to serve others.

Servant presence is not about lowering standards or avoiding hard conversations. It is about choosing proximity over distance and responsibility over privilege. It is the decision to stay engaged with people rather than lead from abstraction.

This is where leadership gets uncomfortable. It is easier to manage roles than to serve people. Easier to issue direction than to notice fatigue, easier to stay above the work than to step into the mess alongside others.

Jesus shows us that leadership credibility is built through presence, not position. Authority that refuses proximity eventually loses trust. Servant presence does not eliminate leadership tension. It transforms it.

The Servant Presence Leadership Framework

Four ways servant leadership shows up in everyday relational leadership.

Notice - Pay Attention to What Others Miss
Jesus noticed dusty feet that everyone else ignored. Servant leaders pay attention to people, not just outcomes. They notice energy, morale, overload, and quiet withdrawal.

Attention is the first act of service.

Lower - Release Status Without Losing Authority
Jesus removed His outer garment. Servant leaders intentionally lay down symbols of superiority that create distance. They do not cling to hierarchy to feel secure.

Lowering yourself does not diminish leadership. It clarifies it.

Serve - Take Responsibility for What Needs Doing
Jesus did the work Himself. Servant leaders do not delegate dignity away. They are willing to step into uncomfortable or unglamorous moments when needed.

Service communicates value more clearly than words.

Model - Show Others How to Lead
Jesus tells His disciples to follow His example. Servant leadership is contagious when it is visible. People imitate what leaders embody, not what they announce.

Modeling sets culture faster than policy.

What This Looks Like at Work

In modern leadership contexts, servant presence rarely looks dramatic.

It looks like leaders who are accessible rather than distant. Leaders who ask questions before issuing directives. Leaders who step into hard conversations instead of avoiding them. Leaders who notice when someone is struggling and respond with care rather than impatience.

In corporate environments, servant presence might show up as leaders who understand frontline realities before setting strategy. In education or ministry, it shows up as leaders who listen without rushing to fix. In trades or operations, it shows up as leaders who respect the work and the people doing it.

Servant leaders do not hover, rescue, or micromanage. They stay close enough to understand what support is actually needed.

Presence does not mean involvement in everything. It means relational availability when it matters.

Reflection

- Where do you tend to rely on position rather than presence?
- What makes you most uncomfortable about serving those you lead?
- How might greater proximity strengthen trust in your leadership?

Scripture to Read

"For even the Son of Man came not to be served but to serve, and to give his life as a ransom for many."
-Mark 10:45 (ESV)

As you reflect on this verse, what does serving "as the Son of Man" look like in your leadership context right now?

Invite God Into This

Take a moment to ask God to show you where He is inviting you closer to people rather than further above them.

Ask for humility that is rooted in confidence, not insecurity. Invite the Holy Spirit to shape how you use authority not to protect yourself, but to care for others well.

Servant leadership begins with willingness.

Take the Next Step

- **Form a habit:** Spend intentional, unhurried time with the people you lead, without an agenda.
- **Have a conversation:** Ask someone on your team what makes their work harder than it needs to be.
- **Choose a new response:** Step into one uncomfortable leadership moment you might normally delegate or avoid.

Servant leadership s not weaken authority. It anchors it.

Good Samaritan - Compassion in Motion Leadership

Love that interrupts

The Moment

Jesus tells the story of the Good Samaritan in response to a question that feels sincere on the surface but reveals a deeper tension underneath.

A lawyer stands and asks, “Teacher, what shall I do to inherit eternal life?” (Luke 10:25, ESV).

Jesus turns the question back on him, grounding the conversation in Scripture: love God with everything you have, and love your neighbor as yourself. The lawyer agrees but then presses further.

“And who is my neighbor?” (Luke 10:29, ESV)

It’s an understandable question. It’s also a revealing one.

At its core, the question is about limits. How far does responsibility extend? Who qualifies for care? Where does obligation end and discretion begin? Jesus answers not with a definition, but with a story.

A man is traveling from Jerusalem to Jericho when he is attacked, stripped, beaten, and left half dead. A priest comes along, sees the man, and passes by. Then a Levite does the same. Both are religious leaders. Both are familiar with the law. Both notice the need and neither intervenes.

Jesus does not speculate about their motives. He simply tells the story. Then a Samaritan enters the scene.

This detail would have immediately unsettled His listeners. Samaritans were despised outsiders culturally, religiously, and socially. Yet Jesus intentionally places the moral weight of the story on this unexpected figure.

"But a Samaritan, as he journeyed, came to where he was, and when he saw him, he had compassion." (Luke 10:33, ESV)

Compassion moves the Samaritan toward the wounded man, not away from him. He stops. He draws close. He tends wounds, transports the man to safety, pays for his care, and commits to follow-up. His compassion is not abstract. It is costly, inconvenient, and sustained.

Jesus ends the story by reframing the original question. He does not ask who qualifies as a neighbor. He asks who *acted* like one.

The Leadership Insight

Compassion, in Scripture, is never treated as a sentiment. It is always expressed through movement.

The priest and the Levite did not fail because they lacked awareness. They failed because they prioritized distance over disruption. Compassion would have required interruption of their schedule, their plans, perhaps even their sense of safety.

This is where leadership tension lives. Most leaders genuinely care about people, but compassion often competes with pace. Schedules are full. Decisions are pressing. Expectations are high. Over time, leaders can unintentionally train themselves to step over need rather than engage it especially when compassion feels inefficient or outside their defined role.

Jesus does not allow that framing. The story of the Good Samaritan dismantles the idea that leadership responsibility can be neatly contained. Compassionate leadership is not driven by convenience, optics, or job description. It is driven by love in motion.

That does not mean leaders abandon boundaries or responsibility. It means they refuse to let productivity numb empathy. It means they recognize that interruption is sometimes the very work God places in front of them.

Growth happens in this discomfort *so that* leaders learn to see people, not just problems.

The Compassion in Motion Leadership Framework

How compassion moves from awareness to action in leadership.

See - Notice Without Avoidance
The Samaritan truly saw the wounded man. He did not look away, rationalize, or delay engagement. Compassion begins with attention. Leaders must be willing to see need clearly, even when it disrupts momentum or challenges assumptions.

Stop - Allow Interruption
Compassion requires pause. The Samaritan stopped his journey and accepted the cost of interruption. Leaders who never slow down eventually lose the ability to lead compassionately.

Stopping is not weakness. It is presence.

Act - Respond Tangibly
Compassion expresses itself through concrete action. The Samaritan did what was necessary, not just what was easy. Leaders demonstrate compassion through practical support, advocacy, and care not just kind words.

Stay - Commit Beyond the Moment
The Samaritan ensured ongoing care. Compassionate leadership does not disappear once the immediate crisis passes. It follows through, protects dignity, and remains engaged long enough for healing to begin.

What This Looks Like at Work

In everyday leadership contexts, compassion in motion rarely looks dramatic. More often, it looks like leaders who choose people over pace in small but meaningful ways.

In corporate environments, it may look like flexibility during a personal crisis, advocacy when systems create unintended harm, or slowing down long enough to understand impact beyond metrics and KPIs.

In education or ministry, it may look like noticing the quiet student or volunteer who is struggling rather than only focusing on the program or outcome.

In construction, operations, or trades, it may look like prioritizing safety, recovery, and dignity even when deadlines press hard.

Compassion does not remove accountability. It shapes how accountability is carried. Leaders who lead without compassion may achieve short-term results, but they erode trust. Leaders who lead with compassion build relational equity that sustains performance over time.

Reflection

- Where do you feel most tempted to bypass compassion in the name of efficiency or responsibility?
- What internal narratives help you justify walking past need?
- How might your leadership rhythms need to shift to make room for compassionate interruption?

Scripture to Read

“Which of these three, do you think, proved to be a neighbor to the man who fell among the robbers?”
-Luke 10:36 (ESV)

As you reflect on this verse, where might Jesus be reframing your understanding of responsibility?

Invite God Into This

Ask God to soften your awareness where it has become dulled by pace, pressure, or routine.

Invite the Holy Spirit to help you see people clearly and respond with wisdom, not avoidance. Pray for discernment to know when to stop, when to act, and when to stay engaged longer than feels convenient.

Compassion is not accidental. It is cultivated.

Take the Next Step

- **Form a habit:** Pause once each day to intentionally notice the people around you, not just the tasks in front of you.
- **Have a conversation:** Check in with someone whose need you might otherwise overlook.
- **Choose a new response:** Choose presence over pace in one situation where interruption feels inconvenient.

Compassion does not weaken leadership. It reveals it.

Barnabas - Encouragement Multiplier Leadership

Belief that unlocks growth

The Moment

Barnabas is not introduced to us by his accomplishments, but by his character. In Acts 4, we learn that his given name is Joseph, but the apostles give him a new name, Barnabas, which means *son of encouragement*.

"Thus Joseph, who was also called by the apostles Barnabas (which means son of encouragement), a Levite, a native of Cyprus..." (Acts 4:36, ESV)

That detail matters. In Scripture, names are not casual. They are revealing. Barnabas is not named for what he achieves, but for how he strengthens others.

We see this most clearly in Acts 9, after Saul's dramatic conversion. Saul (Now Paul) tries to join the disciples in Jerusalem, but fear fills the room. His reputation precedes him because had persecuted believers and no one trusts the transformation yet.

"And when he had come to Jerusalem, he attempted to join the disciples. And they were all afraid of him, for they did not believe that he was a disciple." (Acts 9:26, ESV)

Enter Barnabas.

"But Barnabas took him and brought him to the apostles and declared to them how on the road he had seen the Lord..." (Acts 9:27, ESV)

Barnabas does not minimize Saul's past. He does not deny the risk. He simply chooses to believe that God's work is real and to advocate for what God is doing in someone else.

Later, in Acts 11, when the church in Antioch begins to grow, Barnabas is sent to investigate. When he arrives, Scripture tells us something remarkable:

"When he came and saw the grace of God, he was glad, and he exhorted them all to remain faithful to the Lord with steadfast purpose." (Acts 11:23, ESV)

Barnabas sees grace, and he names it.

The Leadership Insight

Encouragement is one of the most underestimated leadership disciplines. Many leaders assume encouragement is optional, something nice to add once results are achieved. Others confuse encouragement with praise, flattery, or lowering standards. Barnabas shows us something far more robust.

Encouragement is not exaggeration. It is not hype or ignoring weakness. It is not toxic positivity. Encouragement is the disciplined act of naming what God is forming in someone *before* it is fully visible.

Barnabas multiplies leadership not by positioning himself at the center, but by amplifying belief in others. He bridges the gap between potential and opportunity. He creates space for growth by lending credibility where fear would otherwise shut doors.

This is where leadership often fractures. Many leaders wait for proof before offering belief. They demand confidence before granting trust. But Barnabas reverses the sequence. He offers belief *so that* growth can take place.

Encouragement does not replace accountability. It fuels it.

The Encouragement Multiplier Leadership Framework

How encouragement strengthens people without inflating ego or lowering expectations.

See the Work of God - Name What Is Growing
Barnabas looks for evidence of grace. Encouragement begins with discernment, seeing what God is already doing, even when it is fragile or incomplete. Leaders who encourage well are attentive. They notice growth others overlook.

Speak with Courage - Advocate When Others Hesitate
Encouragement often requires risk. Barnabas stakes his credibility on Saul's transformation. Encouraging leaders are willing to stand between fear and opportunity on behalf of others. Silence can stall growth just as easily as criticism.

Create Opportunity - Open Doors, Not Pedestals
Barnabas does not promote Saul to prominence; he creates access. Encouragement is not about spotlighting, it is about removing unnecessary barriers so others can step forward responsibly.

Stay Invested - Walk with People Through Growth
Barnabas does not disappear once opportunity is given. He continues to mentor, support, and partner. Encouragement is not a one-time event. It is a posture over time.

What This Looks Like at Work

In leadership environments today, encouragement multiplier leadership shows up in how leaders talk about people when they are not in the room. It shows up in who gets advocated for in meetings, who is given stretch opportunities, and who is trusted with responsibility before

In corporate contexts, this might look like sponsoring emerging leaders rather than simply evaluating them. In education or ministry, it may look like affirming calling while still shaping competence. In trades or operations, it may look like pairing belief with training and patience.

Encouragement multiplies confidence, not entitlement. When leaders believe in people, people rise to the responsibility placed before them.

Reflection

- Who believed in you before you fully believed in yourself?
- Where might fear be keeping you from advocating for someone else's growth?
- How do you typically balance encouragement and accountability?

Scripture to Read

"Therefore encourage one another and build one another up, just as you are doing."
-1 Thessalonians 5:11 (ESV)

As you reflect on this verse, who might God be inviting you to intentionally build up right now?

Invite God Into This

Ask God to sharpen your eyes to see what He is forming in others.

Invite the Holy Spirit to help you speak courageously, especially when belief feels risky. Pray for wisdom to encourage without inflating ego and to challenge without discouraging heart.

Encouragement, when done well, is an act of faith.

Take the Next Step

- **Form a habit:** Name specific growth you see in one person each day.
- **Have a conversation:** Advocate for someone's development in a room where decisions are made.
- **Choose a new response:** Replace silence with encouragement when growth is evident but unfinished.

Encouragement does not create dependence. It creates momentum.

Aaron & Hur - Shared Load Leadership

Strength that lasts is never carried alone

The Moment

The story unfolds during a moment of intense vulnerability for the Israelites. In Exodus 17, Israel is attacked by the Amalekites shortly after leaving Egypt. They are tired, newly free, and still learning how to trust God outside of slavery. Moses, their leader, is instructed to stand on the hill with the staff of God in his hand while Joshua leads the battle below.

“Whenever Moses held up his hand, Israel prevailed, and whenever he lowered his hand, Amalek prevailed.” (Exodus 17:11, ESV)

At first glance, the dynamic seems straightforward: raised hands mean victory. Lowered hands mean defeat. But the story quickly complicates. Moses grows tired.

His arms cannot stay lifted indefinitely. No amount of calling or authority changes the reality of human limitation. Victory depends not on Moses’ role, but on whether his strength can be sustained.

That is when Aaron and Hur step in.

"So they took a stone and put it under him, and he sat on it, while Aaron and Hur held up his hands, one on one side, and the other on the other side." (Exodus 17:12, ESV)

The battle is won, not because Moses tries harder, but because leadership becomes shared.

The Leadership Insight

This story confronts one of the most persistent falsehoods in leadership: that strong leaders carry the weight alone.

Many leaders are implicitly rewarded for endurance, availability, and self-sufficiency. Over time, strength becomes equated with capacity to hold everything personally. Asking for help feels like weakness. Needing support feels like failure.

Scripture tells a different story.

Moses is not corrected for needing help. He is not replaced. He is supported. The victory does not require him to step down, it requires him to sit down and allow others to hold him up.

Shared load leadership recognizes that leadership is sustained through relationship, not resilience alone. Growth happens in this discomfort *so that* leaders learn to release control and receive support without shame.

The Shared Load Leadership Framework

How leaders create sustainability through shared responsibility.

Acknowledge Limits - Name What You Cannot Carry Alone
Moses' arms grew tired. Leaders must acknowledge limits honestly. Ignoring capacity does not honor God; it tempts burnout.

Acknowledging limits is not abdication. It is wisdom.

Invite Support - Allow Others to Step In
Aaron and Hur do not force themselves into the moment. They are invited by necessity. Leaders must allow others to help, even when pride resists.

Support offered but refused still leaves leaders depleted.

Create Stability - Build Structures That Sustain
The stone beneath Moses matters. Support is not only relational; it is structural. Leaders need systems, rhythms, and practices that reduce unnecessary strain.

Sustainable leadership is designed, not improvised.

Share Victory - Honor Collective Faithfulness
The victory belongs to the people, not one leader. Shared leadership recognizes contribution broadly and resists hero narratives.

Celebrated leaders who refuse to share credit quietly erode trust.

What This Looks Like at Work

In modern leadership contexts, shared load leadership shows up when leaders distribute responsibility thoughtfully rather than hoarding decision-making. It looks like asking for help before exhaustion forces it. It looks like trusting others with meaningful work, not just tasks.

In corporate settings, this may look like collaborative leadership models or shared accountability for outcomes. In education or ministry, it may involve team teaching, co-leading, or mutual pastoral care. In trades or operations, it may involve safety partners, cross-training, and clear handoffs.

Leaders who refuse support eventually limit growth, not just their own, but their team's. Shared load leadership does not slow progress. It sustains it.

Reflection

- Where are you currently carrying leadership weight alone that could be shared?
- What beliefs make it difficult for you to ask for or receive support?
- Who might God be inviting you to trust more fully?

Scripture to Read

"Bear one another's burdens, and so fulfill the law of Christ."
-Galatians 6:2 (ESV)

As you reflect on this verse, what burden might you need to share rather than carry silently?

Invite God Into This

Ask God to reveal where pride or fear may be keeping you isolated.

Invite the Holy Spirit to help you receive support with humility and gratitude. Pray for discernment to know when to stand firm and when to sit down so others can hold you up.

Leadership that lasts is never solo.

Take the Next Step

- **Form a habit:** Name one area of leadership where you intentionally invite collaboration.
- **Have a conversation:** Ask someone you trust what support they see you needing.
- **Choose a new response:** Stop doing one task that could be shared or delegated.

Leadership is not proven by how much you can carry. It is revealed by how well you share the load.

Body of Christ - Interdependent Team Leadership

Strength through difference, not sameness

The Moment

Paul's metaphor of the body emerges not in a moment of unity, but of tension. The church in Corinth was fractured. People were comparing gifts, elevating certain roles, and dismissing others as less important. Spiritual maturity had become tangled with visibility, and difference was being treated as deficiency.

Paul addresses this directly in 1 Corinthians 12. Rather than correcting individual behavior first, he reframes how the community understands itself.

"For just as the body is one and has many members, and all the members of the body, though many, are one body, so it is with Christ." (1 Corinthians 12:12, ESV)

This is not poetic imagery for comfort. It is a corrective framework. Paul emphasizes that the body does not thrive through sameness, hierarchy, or uniform strength. It thrives through interdependence.

Each part matters not because it is impressive, but because it is necessary.

“The eye cannot say to the hand, ‘I have no need of you,’ nor again the head to the feet, ‘I have no need of you.’” (1 Corinthians 12:21, ESV)

The language is unmistakable. Dismissal, whether subtle or explicit, fractures the body.

The Leadership Insight

Many teams struggle not because people lack talent, but because they misunderstand contribution.

Modern leadership cultures often reward visibility, speed, and dominance. Certain roles are celebrated. Others are quietly minimized. Over time, teams begin to believe that some contributions matter more than others, and that belief shapes behavior.

Interdependent leadership challenges this mindset at its root. Paul’s teaching dismantles comparison, hierarchy-driven worth, and the illusion of self-sufficiency. No leader, no role, no function is complete on its own. Teams thrive not when everyone does the same thing well, but when everyone contributes faithfully within their design.

This is uncomfortable for many leaders. Interdependence requires relinquishing control. It requires valuing contributions that do not mirror our own. It requires trusting others to bring strength where we are weak.

Growth happens in this discomfort *so that* teams move from competition to collaboration.

The Interdependent Team Leadership Framework

Four practices that build healthy, interdependent teams.

Honor Difference - Value Distinct Contribution
Paul emphasizes that difference is not a problem to solve; it is a design to honor. Leaders must actively affirm varied strengths, working styles, and roles.

Uniformity weakens teams. Diversity of contribution strengthens them.

Clarify Roles - Reduce Friction and Comparison
Confusion about roles creates comparison and resentment. Interdependent teams function best when responsibilities are clear and contributions are understood.

Clarity protects unity.

Resist Hierarchy of Worth - Reject Status-Based Value
Paul is explicit: no part of the body is expendable. Leaders must guard against valuing roles based on visibility or prestige.

Status-based leadership erodes trust and belonging.

Cultivate Mutual Dependence - Normalize Needing One Another
Interdependence thrives when asking for help is normalized. Leaders model this by naming where they rely on others' strengths.

Teams grow healthier when dependence is expected, not hidden.

What This Looks Like at Work

In leadership environments today, interdependent team leadership shows up in how leaders talk about roles and contributions.

In corporate settings, it means valuing support functions alongside revenue drivers. In education or ministry, it means honoring behind-the-scenes work as much as public-facing roles. In trades or operations, it means recognizing that safety, logistics, and follow-through are as critical as execution.

Interdependent leaders do not flatten responsibility. They elevate contribution.

When teams understand how their work fits together, morale improves, trust deepens, and performance stabilizes.

Belonging is not built through sameness. It is built through shared purpose.

Reflection

- Where might comparison be quietly undermining team health?
- Which contributions on your team may be undervalued or overlooked?
- How do you model dependence on others' strengths?

Scripture to Read

"Now you are the body of Christ and individually members of it."
-1 Corinthians 12:27 (ESV)

As you reflect on this verse, how does it reshape your understanding of leadership and contribution?

Invite God Into This

Ask God to show you where your leadership may unintentionally elevate some roles while diminishing others.

Invite the Holy Spirit to cultivate humility, appreciation, and clarity in how you lead your team. Pray for wisdom to build environments where every contribution is honored and aligned to purpose.

Interdependence is not weakness. It is God's design.

Take the Next Step

- **Form a habit:** Regularly name how different roles contribute to shared success.
- **Have a conversation:** Ask team members where they feel most effective, and least seen.
- **Choose a new response:** Adjust one leadership habit that unintentionally reinforces hierarchy of worth.

Strong teams are not built by uniform leaders. They are built by leaders who understand connection.

Proverbs & James - Wise Communication Leadership

Listening before speaking

The Moment

Scripture speaks about words with remarkable consistency and seriousness. From the wisdom literature of Proverbs to the pastoral urgency of James, language is treated not as a soft skill, but as a matter of life, direction, and consequence. Words shape relationships, cultures, and outcomes long before they shape reputations.

Proverbs repeatedly returns to the theme of restraint and discernment:

“When words are many, transgression is not lacking, but whoever restrains his lips is prudent.” (Proverbs 10:19, ESV)

James, writing to believers navigating conflict, pressure, and community tension, echoes this warning with even greater urgency:

"Let every person be quick to hear, slow to speak, slow to anger." (James 1:19, ESV)

James is not offering communication tips. He is offering formation guidance. He understands that speech is rarely neutral. It either builds or erodes trust. It either clarifies or confuses. It either steadies people or escalates them.

This is why James later issues such a strong caution:

"Not many of you should become teachers... for you know that we who teach will be judged with greater strictness." (James 3:1, ESV)

Leadership multiplies the impact of words. The more influence a leader carries, the more weight their language holds.

The Leadership Insight

Most communication breakdowns in leadership are not caused by lack of information. They are caused by lack of restraint.

Leaders often speak quickly because they feel pressure to respond, to clarify, to reassure, or to assert control. Silence can feel risky. Pausing can feel unproductive. Listening can feel passive.

Scripture reframes all three. Wise leaders listen first, not because they lack conviction, but because they value understanding. They speak deliberately, not because they fear conflict, but because they understand the power of timing. They restrain their words, not to withhold truth, but to steward it carefully.

This is where leadership gets uncomfortable. Words feel productive. Silence feels exposed. But Proverbs and James both insist that wisdom is revealed not by volume, but by discernment.

Growth happens in this discomfort *so that* leaders learn to govern their tongues rather than be governed by them.

The Wise Communication Leadership Framework

Four practices that anchor communication in wisdom rather than impulse.

Listen Fully - Seek Understanding Before Response
Listening is not waiting for your turn to speak. It is active attention. Leaders who listen well gather context, emotion, and nuance before responding.

Understanding precedes clarity.

Pause Intentionally - Resist the Urge to React
James pairs slow speech with slow anger for a reason. Reaction often masquerades as decisiveness. Pausing creates space for discernment and prevents unnecessary escalation.

Restraint protects relationship.

Speak Purposefully - Choose Words That Serve
Wise leaders speak with intention. Their words are clear, honest, and measured. They resist exaggeration, sarcasm, and careless phrasing, knowing that tone often carries more weight than content.

Words should move situations forward, not inflame them.

Time Truth Well - Match Message to Moment
Truth spoken without timing can wound rather than heal. Wisdom discerns when to speak, how to speak, and when to wait.

Timing is not avoidance. It is leadership maturity.

What This Looks Like at Work

In leadership environments, wise communication shows up in how leaders handle tension and uncertainty.

In corporate settings, it may look like asking clarifying questions before drawing conclusions, or choosing thoughtful follow-up over immediate reply. In education or ministry, it may look like listening beneath surface behavior to understand underlying need. In trades or operations, it may look like calm, clear instruction under pressure rather than sharp or reactive speech.

Wise communication does not eliminate hard conversations. It improves how those conversations land.

Leaders who speak wisely create cultures of trust, psychological safety, and clarity. Leaders who speak impulsively, even with good intentions, often create confusion or defensiveness.

Reflection

- When do you feel most tempted to speak quickly rather than listen carefully?
- How does pressure affect your tone and word choice?
- Where might restraint strengthen your leadership influence?

Scripture to Read

"Whoever restrains his words has knowledge, and he who has a cool spirit is a man of understanding."
-Proverbs 17:27 (ESV)

As you reflect on this verse, what would it look like to lead with a "cool spirit" in your current context?

Invite God Into This

Ask God to guard your tongue and shape your listening.

Invite the Holy Spirit to slow you down where urgency pushes you to react. Pray for wisdom to know when to speak, when to wait, and how to communicate truth with grace.

Words reveal the heart. Ask God to shape both.

Take the Next Step

- **Form a habit:** Pause before responding in emotionally charged moments.
- **Have a conversation:** Ask one clarifying question before offering your opinion.
- **Choose a new response:** Replace reactive language with deliberate phrasing in one key interaction.

Wise leaders are not silent. They are intentional.

Nathan - Courageous Feedback Leadership

Truth that restores, not shames

The Moment

David is at the height of his power when Nathan comes to him. By this point, David is no longer the shepherd boy. He is king. He has unified Israel, secured Jerusalem, and established himself as God's chosen leader. Outwardly, everything looks strong. Inwardly, something has gone deeply wrong.

David has abused his power, committed adultery with Bathsheba, and arranged the death of her husband, Uriah. The consequences are devastating, but the secrecy is complete, at least on the surface.

Then Nathan arrives.

Nathan does not confront David immediately. He tells a story.

"There were two men in a certain city, the one rich and the other poor." (2 Samuel 12:1, ESV)

The story is simple and unjust. A rich man steals a poor man's only lamb to prepare a meal for a guest. David responds with anger and moral clarity.

"As the LORD lives, the man who has done this deserves to die." (2 Samuel 12:5, ESV)

And then Nathan speaks the words that change everything.

"You are the man!" (2 Samuel 12:7, ESV)

This is not public humiliation. This is not passive aggression. This is courageous, precise truth spoken directly to the person who needs to hear it despite the risk.

Nathan's courage is not reckless. It is faithful.

The Leadership Insight

Courageous feedback is one of the rarest and most necessary forms of leadership. Most leaders either avoid hard feedback or deliver it poorly. Avoidance allows dysfunction to fester. Poor delivery wounds rather than heals. Both are failures of leadership, even when intentions are good.

Nathan shows us a better way. He does not shame David. He does not soften the truth to protect himself. He does not gather allies to build a case. He speaks directly, wisely, and at great personal risk.

This is where leadership courage is tested. Feedback that protects the leader's comfort rather than the community's health is not loving. But feedback that seeks to wound rather than restore is not faithful either.

Nathan's courage is anchored in care for David, for the people, and for God's standards. Growth happens in this discomfort *so that* leaders learn to value restoration over reputation.

The Courageous Feedback Leadership Framework

How truth can be spoken in ways that protect dignity while addressing reality.

Prepare the Ground - Seek Understanding Before Confrontation
Nathan's story invites **Reflection** before accusation. Courageous feedback begins with discernment, not reaction. Leaders must understand the situation fully before speaking.

Preparation protects clarity.

Speak Clearly - Name the Truth Without Blame or Blur
Nathan's words are direct and unmistakable. Courageous feedback avoids vagueness and passive language. It names behavior honestly while refusing to attack identity.

Clarity is an act of respect.

Anchor in Care - Let Relationship Shape Delivery
Nathan speaks because he cares. Courageous feedback is not venting. It is stewardship. When care is absent, truth becomes cruelty.

Love determines tone.

Aim for Restoration - Call People Forward, Not Out
Nathan's goal is repentance and restoration, not exposure. Courageous feedback always points toward what can be rebuilt.

Correction without hope leads to despair.

What This Looks Like at Work

In leadership environments today, courageous feedback shows up when leaders address issues early rather than letting resentment accumulate. It shows up when conversations are honest, timely, and grounded in care rather than frustration.

In corporate settings, this may look like addressing behavior that undermines trust instead of tolerating it for performance. In education or ministry, it may look like naming misalignment while reaffirming calling. In trades or operations, it may look like correcting unsafe practices directly to protect people rather than avoiding conflict.

Courageous feedback does not guarantee immediate agreement. It builds long-term trust.

Leaders who refuse to speak truth eventually lose credibility. Leaders who speak truth carelessly lose people. Courageous leaders do neither.

Reflection

- Where are you currently avoiding a conversation that needs to happen?
- What fears make courageous feedback feel risky for you?
- How do you typically balance honesty and care when addressing difficult issues?

Scripture to Read

"Faithful are the wounds of a friend; profuse are the kisses of an enemy."
-Proverbs 27:6 (ESV)

As you reflect on this verse, how does it reshape your understanding of loving leadership?

Invite God Into This

Ask God for courage that is anchored in love rather than fear.

Invite the Holy Spirit to guide your words, your timing, and your tone. Pray for wisdom to speak truth that restores rather than shames, and humility to receive feedback when it is offered to you.

Truth spoken in love is a gift.

Take the Next Step

- **Form a habit:** Reflect before difficult conversations rather than reacting emotionally.
- **Have a conversation:** Address one issue you've been avoiding with clarity and care.
- **Choose a new response:** Replace indirect communication with respectful honesty.

Courageous feedback does not damage leadership. It strengthens it.

Acts 2 - Sustaining Rhythms Leadership

Habits that hold people together

The Moment

Acts 2 is often remembered for its dramatic opening, the sound of a mighty rushing wind, tongues of fire, and bold proclamation. But Luke does not end the chapter with spectacle. He ends it with structure.

After the crowds disperse and the excitement settles, we are given a picture of how the early church actually lived.

"And they devoted themselves to the apostles' teaching and the fellowship, to the breaking of bread and the prayers." (Acts 2:42, ESV)

That word *devoted* matters. It implies consistency, intention, and commitment over time. Luke continues:

"And all who believed were together and had all things in common... And day by day, attending the temple together and breaking bread in their homes..." (Acts 2:44, 46, ESV)

This is not an accidental community. It is a rhythmic one. Teaching, fellowship, meals, prayer, generosity, and shared time are woven into daily and weekly life.

These practices are not flashy. They are repeatable. And they form the relational infrastructure that sustains the church long after the moment passes.

The Leadership Insight

Healthy relationships are not sustained by occasional connection. They are sustained by shared rhythm.

Many leaders underestimate the power of consistency. They focus on peak moments like retreats, launches, initiatives, celebrations while neglecting the everyday practices that actually hold teams together. Over time, relationships begin to feel thin, reactive, or transactional, even when intentions are good.

Acts 2 offers a different vision. The early church does not rely on charisma or constant novelty. It relies on devotion to shared practices. These rhythms create trust, predictability, and belonging. People know when they will gather, how they will engage, and what matters most.

This is where leadership maturity shows up. Sustaining rhythms require patience and repetition. They require leaders to value formation over frenzy and resist the temptation to constantly reinvent rather than deepen.

Growth happens in this discipline *so that* teams remain connected when energy fluctuates and seasons change.

The Sustaining Rhythms Leadership Framework

Four rhythms that anchor healthy teams over time.

Gather Regularly - Protect Shared Time
The early believers gathered consistently. Leaders who sustain relationships protect time for connection, not just productivity. Regular gathering communicates priority and care.

What is protected becomes trusted.

Anchor Learning - Return to Shared Truth
Teaching was central to the community. Leaders create stability by grounding teams in shared purpose, values, and understanding. This may look like vision, mission, Scripture, standards, or principles but it must be consistent.

Shared truth creates alignment.

Break Bread - Build Relational Warmth
Meals matter in Acts 2. Shared space outside of formal work builds trust and humanizes leadership. Leaders who make room for relational connection strengthen cohesion.

Belonging grows in ordinary moments.

Practice Together - Normalize Spiritual and Relational Habits
Prayer and generosity are practiced communally. Leaders shape culture by normalizing habits that reinforce trust, humility, and dependence on God.

Rhythms form culture more reliably than speeches.

What This Looks Like at Work

In leadership environments today, sustaining rhythms show up in the patterns leaders establish and maintain.

In corporate contexts, this may look like consistent check-ins, team learning rhythms, shared reflection, or predictable feedback cycles, whether those are KPIs, standards, learning outcomes, or progress markers. In education or ministry, it may look like regular gathering, shared prayer, and intentional discipleship rhythms. In trades or operations, it may look like safety huddles, consistent communication practices, and shared accountability rhythms.

Sustaining rhythms reduce anxiety because people know what to expect.

When **rhythm is absent**, leaders compensate with urgency. When **rhythm is present**, leaders build trust quietly over time.

Reflection

- What rhythms currently shape the relationships on your team?
- Where does inconsistency create friction or fatigue?
- What practices might need to be simplified or protected to sustain connection?

Scripture to Read

"And the Lord added to their number day by day those who were being saved."
-Acts 2:47 (ESV)

As you reflect on this verse, how might faithfulness to rhythm prepare space for growth beyond what you can control?

Invite God Into This

Ask God to help you see which rhythms are life-giving and which are draining.

Invite the Holy Spirit to guide you toward practices that sustain people, not just performance. Pray for wisdom to lead patiently, trusting that steady faithfulness produces lasting fruit.

Rhythm is not rigidity. It is care expressed over time.

Take the Next Step

- **Form a habit:** Identify one rhythm you will protect consistently.
- **Have a conversation:** Ask your team what rhythms help them feel connected and supported.
- **Choose a new response:** Remove or simplify one practice that adds noise without adding value.

Leadership is not sustained by intensity. It is sustained by devotion.

Stage 3 | Lead Leaders - Multiplication

Direction that Reproduces Leadership

By the end of **Stage 2**, something important has shifted.

You have learned how to lead yourself with integrity and discernment. You have learned how to lead a team with presence, care, courage, and rhythm. You have built trust through relationship and consistency, not intensity.

And now leadership asks something more of you.

Not *How do I lead well personally?*
Not *How do I lead a team effectively?*
But *How do I multiply leadership through others?*

This is the transition from addition to multiplication.

Leading a team is largely about proximity, being close enough to model, support, encourage, and correct. Leading leaders requires a different posture. Influence extends further. Decisions ripple wider and direction matters more than activity. What you say, prioritize, and release begins to shape leaders who will, in turn, shape others.

This stage is not about doing more. It is about stewarding influence so leadership outlives your direct involvement. Healthy relationships create stability, but leadership does not stop at stability. At some point, leaders must step into direction not just for themselves, but for those they are developing and sending forward.

This is where many leaders feel tension. Multiplication introduces risk. You cannot control every outcome. You cannot stay equally close to everyone. You must trust leaders to carry responsibility, make decisions, and sometimes get it wrong. For leaders accustomed to hands-on influence, this can feel unsettling.

Scripture does not shy away from this tension. Throughout the Bible, God consistently works through multiplication. Moses raises up Joshua. Elijah prepares Elisha. Jesus forms the Twelve and then sends them out. Paul invests deeply in a few so the gospel can spread widely.

Multiplication is not abdication. It is intentional development paired with release.

Stage 3 is about discerning direction, clarifying vision, and empowering others to lead faithfully in their own contexts. It is about making decisions with incomplete information, communicating purpose without coercion, and trusting God to work through leaders you no longer directly manage.

This stage will explore how leaders:

- Discern God's direction amid complexity and change,
- Cast vision that aligns rather than controls,
- Release authority while maintaining accountability,
- Develop leaders who can lead others,
- Navigate uncertainty with faith and clarity.

Vision detached from character becomes control.
Vision disconnected from relationship becomes coercion.

But **vision entrusted** to formed leaders becomes multiplication.

Stage 3 builds directly on what has come before.

Leaders who have learned to lead themselves and lead teams are now prepared to lead leaders, not by having all the answers, but by stewarding clarity, conviction, and trust in motion.

This is the stage where leadership begins to outgrow proximity. Not because leaders pull away, but because they intentionally send others forward.

Let's lead leaders.

Abraham - Faith-Forward Leadership

Obedience before clarity

The Moment

Abraham's leadership story does not begin with a plan. It begins with a call. In Genesis 12, Abram is living a settled life in Haran when God interrupts it with a directive that is as clear as it is incomplete.

"Go from your country and your kindred and your father's house to the land that I will show you." (Genesis 12:1, ESV)

God does not provide a map, explain the timeline or outline the risks and rewards. He simply calls Abram to leave what is familiar and move toward what is unknown and what follows is striking in its simplicity.

"So Abram went, as the LORD had told him." (Genesis 12:4, ESV)

That sentence carries enormous weight. Abram does not negotiate. He does not delay until certainty arrives. He moves forward in obedience, trusting that direction will come *as he goes*, not before.

This is the foundation of faith-forward leadership.

The Leadership Insight

Multiplication always begins with obedience, not certainty. Leaders who are moving from leading teams to leading leaders often feel an increased pressure to be right. Decisions affect more people. Influence extends further and the cost of mistakes feels heavier. As a result, leaders can become hesitant and want to wait for perfect clarity before taking the next step.

Abraham's story dismantles that approach. God does not ask Abraham to understand everything. He asks him to trust and move. Direction is revealed through obedience, not analysis. Vision unfolds through faithfulness, not control.

This is deeply uncomfortable for many leaders. We prefer clarity before commitment. We want guarantees before movement and we want to know outcomes before we act. But Scripture consistently shows that God forms leaders by calling them forward before the path is fully visible.

Growth happens in this tension *so that* leaders learn to trust God more than their own certainty.

The Faith-Forward Leadership Framework

How leaders move faithfully without full visibility.

Listen - Receive Direction Without Demanding Detail
Abraham hears God's call and responds. Faith-forward leaders learn to listen for direction without insisting on full explanation. They discern God's voice through Scripture, prayer, and wise counsel, even when details remain incomplete.

Listening requires surrender.

Leave - Release What Is Familiar
God calls Abraham to leave his country, people, and patterns. Faith-forward leadership requires letting go-of comfort, reputation, and predictable outcomes. Leaders cannot multiply if they cling to what no longer fits the next season.

Leaving is an act of trust.

Move - Obey Before Certainty Arrives
Abraham goes. Movement matters. Faith-forward leaders step into action without waiting for perfect conditions. Obedience creates momentum; hesitation stalls it.

Movement reveals direction.

Trust - Build Altars Along the Way
Throughout his journey, Abraham builds altars to the Lord (Genesis 12:7–8). Faith-forward leaders pause to remember God's faithfulness as they move. Trust is strengthened through remembrance, not results.

Trust grows through worship.

What This Looks Like at Work

In leadership environments today, faith-forward leadership shows up when leaders make principled decisions without having every variable resolved.

In corporate settings, this may look like committing to a strategic direction while remaining adaptable as information unfolds, whether measured through KPIs, outcomes, standards, or learning benchmarks. In ministry or education, it may look like stepping into a calling before resources feel sufficient. In trades or operations, it may look like adopting safer or more ethical practices before immediate payoff is visible.

Faith-forward leadership does not mean recklessness. It means alignment.

Leaders move not because the path is easy, but because obedience is clear.

Reflection

- Where are you currently waiting for clarity that may only come after movement?
- What familiar patterns or comforts might God be asking you to release?
- How do you typically respond when direction feels incomplete?

Scripture to Read

"By faith Abraham obeyed when he was called to go out... And he went out, not knowing where he was going."
-Hebrews 11:8 (ESV)

As you reflect on this verse, what does obedience look like for you right now?

Invite God Into This

Ask God to help you listen without fear and move without needing guarantees.

Invite the Holy Spirit to strengthen your trust where uncertainty feels heavy. Pray for courage to take the next faithful step, even when the destination is not yet clear.

Faith does not eliminate risk. It anchors obedience.

Take the Next Step

- **Form a habit:** Spend time discerning direction through prayer and Scripture before seeking solutions.
- **Have a conversation:** Ask a trusted leader where they see God inviting you forward.
- **Choose a new response:** Take one concrete step in obedience rather than waiting for perfect clarity.

Leadership multiplication does not begin with answers. It begins with faith.

Nehemiah - Burdened Vision Leadership

Vision that begins with grief

The Moment

Nehemiah does not begin his leadership journey with a strategy session or a bold declaration. It begins with a conversation. While serving as cupbearer to the king of Persia, Nehemiah asks about the condition of Jerusalem which is the city of his ancestors. The report is devastating.

“The remnant there in the province who had survived the exile is in great trouble and shame. The wall of Jerusalem is broken down, and its gates are destroyed by fire.” (Nehemiah 1:3, ESV)

Nehemiah’s response is not immediate action.

“As soon as I heard these words I sat down and wept and mourned for days, and I continued fasting and praying before the God of heaven.” (Nehemiah 1:4, ESV)

That pause matters.

Nehemiah does not rush to fix the problem. He allows the weight of it to settle. He lets grief do its work. He prays, he fasts and he listens. Only after this season of burden does vision begin to form.

When Nehemiah eventually speaks to the king, his words are measured, clear, and grounded. The vision has been shaped long before it is spoken.

The Leadership Insight

Not all vision begins with excitement. Some vision begins with sorrow. Many leaders assume vision must feel energizing from the start. They look for inspiration, momentum, or clarity before committing. Nehemiah offers a different model.

God often births vision through burden. A holy burden is not frustration or irritation. It is a sustained weight that will not lift. It draws leaders toward prayer rather than reaction. It clarifies responsibility rather than inflaming ego. It aligns leaders with God's heart before it mobilizes others.

This is especially critical when leading leaders. Multiplication requires discernment. Leaders must distinguish between ideas that excite them and burdens God is inviting them to carry. Vision driven by ego demands followers. Vision shaped by burden invites partnership.

Growth happens in this waiting *so that* leaders lead from alignment rather than impulse.

The Burdened Vision Leadership Framework

How vision forms through prayerful discernment rather than urgency.

Receive the Burden - Allow Yourself to Be Moved
Nehemiah does not numb himself to the news. He allows grief to settle. Leaders who multiply well resist the urge to fix immediately. They let concern become conviction.

Burden clarifies calling.

Pray Before Proposing - Seek God's Heart First
Nehemiah spends time fasting and praying. Vision formed without prayer often reflects preference rather than purpose. Leaders must ask not just *What is wrong?* but *What is mine to carry?*

Prayer refines vision.

Wait for Alignment - Discern Timing and Favor
Months pass before Nehemiah speaks to the king. Vision does not need to be rushed. Leaders who wait for alignment protect credibility and sustainability.

Timing matters.

Invite Ownership - Cast Vision That Mobilizes Others
When Nehemiah finally speaks, he invites others into the work rather than positioning himself as the hero.

"Come, let us build the wall of Jerusalem, that we may no longer suffer derision." (Nehemiah 2:17, ESV)

Vision multiplies when it creates shared responsibility.

What This Looks Like at Work

In leadership environments today, burdened vision leadership shows up when leaders take time to discern before declaring direction.

In corporate contexts, this may look like sitting with data, stories, and impact before launching initiatives, whether those are measured through KPIs, outcomes, learning standards, or safety benchmarks. In education or ministry, it may look like listening deeply to students, families, or communities before redesigning programs. In trades or operations, it may look like recognizing systemic issues and addressing root causes rather than symptoms.

Burdened vision does not rush people. It invites them. Leaders who skip the burden often struggle to sustain momentum. Leaders who carry the burden faithfully create alignment that lasts.

Reflection

- What issues consistently weigh on your heart rather than passing quickly?
- Where might God be asking you to sit longer with a burden rather than act immediately?
- How do you distinguish between personal frustration and holy responsibility?

Scripture to Read

"O Lord, let your ear be attentive to the prayer of your servant."
-Nehemiah 1:11 (ESV)

As you reflect on this verse, what burden might God be inviting you to bring to Him more consistently?

Invite God Into This

Ask God to reveal what burdens He is placing on your heart.

Invite the Holy Spirit to help you discern which concerns are yours to carry and which are not. Pray for patience to wait, courage to act when the time is right, and humility to invite others into the work.

Vision shaped by prayer is vision that lasts.

Take the Next Step

- **Form a habit:** Spend time praying over concerns before trying to solve them.
- **Have a conversation:** Ask a trusted leader what burdens they see you carrying well.
- **Choose a new response:** Delay one decision long enough to seek alignment rather than urgency.

Multiplication begins with burden, not bravado.

Moses - Anchored Decision Leadership

Choosing obedience amid complexity

The Moment

Moses stands between God and the people more often than any leader would choose. In Exodus 32, he comes down from Mount Sinai carrying the tablets of the covenant only to find chaos below. The people, anxious and impatient, have pressured Aaron into creating a golden calf. Worship has turned reckless. Leadership has fractured and trust has been violated.

“When Moses saw that the people had broken loose... he stood in the gate of the camp and said, ‘Who is on the LORD’s side? Come to me.’” (Exodus 32:25–26, ESV)

This is not a popular moment. Moses does not soften the decision. He does not attempt to manage optics or preserve comfort. He draws a clear line and calls for alignment.

But this is not the only moment that defines Moses' leadership. Again and again, Moses is required to decide amid competing voices, God's instruction, the people's demands, fear of failure, exhaustion, and the weight of responsibility. He intercedes, he waits, he acts, he listens. He holds tension rather than collapsing under it.

Anchored decision-making becomes his defining leadership discipline.

The Leadership Insight

Leaders who lead leaders must make decisions that others will carry forward. That reality changes the weight of decision-making. When leaders are close to the work, they can course-correct quickly. When leaders are leading leaders, decisions shape direction long after the moment has passed.

This is where many leaders struggle. Pressure mounts from every side; data, urgency, expectations, opinions, and fear of consequences. Without anchors, leaders begin to drift. They overreact to noise. They avoid hard decisions. Or they default to what feels safest rather than what is faithful.

Moses shows us another way. Anchored leaders decide from conviction rooted in God's presence, not from reaction to pressure. They discern before they declare. They listen carefully, then act decisively.

Growth happens in this tension *so that* leaders learn to trust God's direction more than popular opinion.

The Anchored Decision Leadership Framework

How leaders make decisions that hold steady amid complexity.

Return to God's Presence - Anchor Before Acting
Moses regularly returns to the tent of meeting. Anchored decisions are not made in isolation from God. Leaders must cultivate rhythms of prayer and reflection that ground them before action.

Presence precedes clarity.

Weigh with Wisdom - Discern Competing Voices
Moses listens to God, hears the people, and considers counsel, but he does not treat all voices as equal. Anchored leaders discern which voices inform and which distract.

Wisdom filters noise.

Draw Clear Boundaries - Decide Without Apology
Moses draws lines when necessary. Anchored leadership requires clarity. Decisions must be communicated clearly and upheld consistently, even when they are unpopular.

Clarity creates stability.

Trust God with Outcomes - Obey Even When Costly
Moses cannot control results. Anchored leaders release outcomes to God. Obedience matters more than approval.

Faithfulness outweighs comfort.

What This Looks Like at Work

In leadership environments today, anchored decision leadership shows up when leaders resist urgency-driven choices and instead decide from principle.

In corporate settings, this may look like prioritizing long-term integrity over short-term gain whether measured through KPIs, outcomes, compliance standards, or learning metrics. In education or ministry, it may look like holding to values when pressure pushes toward compromise. In trades or operations, it may look like choosing safety and quality over speed.

Anchored decisions build trust over time even when they create discomfort in the moment.

Leaders who waver erode confidence. Leaders who decide from conviction create stability for those who follow.

Reflection

- Where do you feel the most pressure to compromise clarity for comfort?
- What voices most influence your decisions under stress?
- How do you currently anchor your decision-making in God's presence?

Scripture to Read

"The LORD is my strength and my song, and he has become my salvation."
-Exodus 15:2 (ESV)

As you reflect on this verse, what does it mean to draw strength from God rather than from certainty?

Invite God Into This

Ask God to anchor your leadership in His presence rather than pressure.

Invite the Holy Spirit to help you discern which voices deserve weight and which should be released. Pray for courage to decide faithfully, even when outcomes are unclear or costly.

Anchored leaders do not rush. They remain steady.

Take the Next Step

- **Form a habit:** Pause before major decisions to seek God's guidance intentionally.
- **Have a conversation:** Ask a trusted leader how they discern decisions under pressure.
- **Choose a new response:** Replace reactive decision-making with deliberate discernment in one area.

Leaders who anchor decisions create direction others can trust.

Jesus Sends the Twelve - Release & Trust Leadership

Authority shared, not hoarded

The Moment

By the time Jesus sends out the Twelve, He has already done significant work *with* them. They have watched Him teach, heal, confront, withdraw, and pray. They have asked questions, misunderstood parables, argued about status, and witnessed miracles they cannot yet fully explain. They are far from finished but they are ready to be sent.

In Matthew 10, Jesus does something decisive.

"And he called to him his twelve disciples and gave them authority over unclean spirits, to cast them out, and to heal every disease and every affliction." (Matthew 10:1, ESV)

That word *authority* is critical.

Jesus does not simply give them tasks. He gives them authority. And then He sends them out without staying close enough to correct every misstep or clarify every question in real time.

He also gives them instructions that feel risky.

"Take no bag for your journey, or two tunics or sandals or a staff..." (Luke 9:3, ESV)

Jesus sends them light, dependent, and exposed. This is not negligence. It is intentional formation.

The Leadership Insight

Multiplication requires release. Leaders who are effective at leading teams often struggle here. Proximity has been their strength. Involvement has been their instinct. They know how to support, correct, and adjust in real time.

But leading leaders requires a different discipline. At some point, leaders must trust what has been formed rather than controlling what unfolds. They must allow others to lead imperfectly, knowing that growth often comes through responsibility, not observation.

Jesus models this with remarkable clarity. He does not wait until the disciples are flawless. He sends them while they are still learning. He trusts the authority He has given more than the certainty of outcomes.

This is deeply uncomfortable. Release introduces risk. Leaders cannot manage perception, execution, or results the way they once could. Mistakes become visible. Outcomes become shared. Control is exchanged for trust. Growth happens in this vulnerability *so that* leadership multiplies rather than bottlenecks.

The Release & Trust Leadership Framework

How leaders move from control to multiplication without disengagement.

Clarify Authority - Name What Has Been Entrusted
Jesus clearly gives authority before sending. Leaders must be explicit about what others are empowered to decide and carry. Ambiguity creates fear and hesitation.

Clarity builds confidence.

Release Control - Step Back Without Abandoning Care
Jesus sends the disciples without hovering. Leaders release involvement while remaining relationally available. Release is not absence. It is restraint.

Trust requires distance.

Expect Growth Through Responsibility - Allow Learning in Motion
The disciples will get things wrong. Jesus knows this. Leaders must allow responsibility to become the teacher rather than rescuing prematurely.

Competence grows through ownership.

Receive Them Back - Debrief, Restore, and Recommission
When the disciples return, Jesus listens to their reports and helps them process what happened (Luke 9:10). Release is paired with reflection, not judgment.

Trust deepens through learning.

What This Looks Like at Work

In leadership environments today, release and trust leadership shows up when leaders stop being the decision bottleneck.

In corporate contexts, this may look like empowering leaders to make decisions within clear guardrails measured through outcomes, KPIs, standards, or learning goals without constant approval loops. In education or ministry, it may look like sending leaders to shepherd others without micromanagement. In trades or operations, it may look like trusting trained leaders with safety, quality, and execution decisions in real time.

Release does not remove accountability. It relocates it.

Leaders who **refuse to release** eventually limit scale. Leaders who **release wisely** create space for growth that outpaces them.

Reflection

- Where are you still holding control that could be entrusted to others?
- What fears surface when you consider releasing authority?
- How do you currently support learning without rescuing?

Scripture to Read

"Whoever receives you receives me, and whoever receives me receives him who sent me."
-Matthew 10:40 (ESV)

As you reflect on this verse, what does it mean to trust others to represent what you value?

Invite God Into This

Ask God to reveal where fear or pride may be limiting your willingness to release authority.

Invite the Holy Spirit to help you trust what He has formed in others. Pray for wisdom to release with clarity, support with humility, and correct with grace.

Multiplication requires faith in God's work beyond your direct control.

Take the Next Step

- **Form a habit:** Clearly name decision authority for one leader you are developing.
- **Have a conversation:** Ask a leader what support they need to carry responsibility well.
- **Choose a new response:** Stop stepping in where ownership has already been given.

Leadership multiplication does not happen through control. It happens through trust.

Elijah & Elisha - Successor-Shaping Leadership

Preparing others to carry what you cannot

The Moment

Elijah's story is often remembered for fire from heaven, bold confrontation, and dramatic miracles. But one of the most important moments of his leadership happens quietly, on the road, as his ministry nears its end.

God tells Elijah that his season is closing and that Elisha will follow him.

"You shall anoint Elisha the son of Shaphat… and he shall be prophet in your place." (1 Kings 19:16, ESV)

Elijah does not resist this instruction. He does not cling to relevance or delay obedience. Instead, he goes and finds Elisha at work in the fields. Without fanfare, Elijah throws his cloak (his mantle) over Elisha's shoulders.

This is not symbolic theater. It is a transfer of calling. Elisha responds by leaving his former life behind. He burns his plow, sacrifices his oxen, and follows Elijah fully. From that moment on, Elisha serves, watches, learns, and walks closely with Elijah.

Years later, as Elijah's departure approaches, Elisha refuses to leave his side.

"As the LORD lives, and as you yourself live, I will not leave you." (2 Kings 2:2, ESV)

When the moment comes, Elijah asks Elisha what he desires.

"Please let there be a double portion of your spirit on me." (2 Kings 2:9, ESV)

This is not ambition. It is responsibility. And when Elijah is taken up, the mantle falls.

"He picked up the cloak of Elijah that had fallen from him..." (2 Kings 2:13, ESV)

Succession is complete not because Elijah stayed forever, but because he prepared someone else to continue the work.

The Leadership Insight

Many leaders are good at developing support. Far fewer are intentional about shaping successors. Support helps leaders do their work. Successors carry the work forward.

This distinction matters deeply in multiplication. Leaders who avoid succession often do so unintentionally. They mentor broadly but prepare no one deeply. They delegate tasks but withhold authority. They fear becoming unnecessary or losing influence. Over time, leadership becomes centralized and fragile.

Elijah models a different posture. He identifies a successor early. He allows proximity over time. He invites Elisha into the full reality of leadership, its cost, its loneliness, its faith. And when the moment comes, he releases the mantle fully.

Growth happens in this relinquishment *so that* leadership outlives the leader.

The Successor-Shaping Leadership Framework

How leaders intentionally prepare others to lead beyond them.

Identify Early - See Who God Is Forming
Elijah does not wait until the end to notice Elisha. Leaders who multiply well pay attention to faithfulness, teachability, and endurance not just talent.

Succession begins with discernment.

Invite Close Proximity - Allow Access, Not Just Assignment
Elisha walks with Elijah for years. Successors need proximity to observe decision-making, values, and faith under pressure. Development without access stays shallow.

Closeness shapes competence.

Transfer Authority - Release Responsibility Gradually
The mantle represents authority, not just mentorship. Leaders must intentionally transfer responsibility, allowing successors to lead while support is still available.

Authority must be practiced, not promised.

Release Fully - Let the Work Continue Without You
Elijah does not linger. He allows the mantle to fall and trusts God with the outcome. True succession requires leaders to step aside without undermining what follows.

Release completes multiplication.

What This Looks Like at Work

In leadership environments today, successor-shaping leadership shows up when leaders move beyond development programs and into intentional handoff.

In corporate contexts, this may look like identifying and preparing future leaders well before transitions occur, pairing responsibility with mentoring and exposure to decision-making. In education or ministry, it may look like discipling leaders who can shepherd others independently. In trades or operations, it may look like training and empowering others to carry technical, safety, or leadership responsibility fully.

Organizations that fail to plan succession become dependent on personalities. Organizations that shape successors build resilience.

Reflection

- Who might God be inviting you to prepare as a successor rather than just a helper?
- Where might fear or identity be making it hard to release leadership?
- How are you intentionally transferring authority, not just knowledge?

Scripture to Read

"Elisha said, 'Let me inherit a double portion of your spirit.'"
-2 Kings 2:9 (ESV)

As you reflect on this verse, what responsibility might God be inviting you to entrust to someone else?

Invite God Into This

Ask God to reveal where you may be holding leadership too tightly.

Invite the Holy Spirit to help you see others as future carriers of the work, not just supporters of it. Pray for humility to prepare successors faithfully and courage to release when the time comes.

Leadership that multiplies must eventually let go.

Take the Next Step

- **Form a habit:** Intentionally invest in one leader beyond immediate need.
- **Have a conversation:** Ask someone you are developing what responsibility they feel ready to carry.
- **Choose a new response:** Share decision-making authority where you normally retain it.

Leadership is not measured by how long you hold the mantle. It is measured by whether it falls into capable hands.

Paul - Guarded Influence Leadership

Leading without proximity

The Moment

Much of Paul's leadership unfolds at a distance. While Acts records his travels, many of Paul's most formative leadership moments come not from presence, but from absence. He plants churches, raises leaders, and then leaves, sometimes by choice, sometimes by force. Persecution, imprisonment, geography, and calling all limit his physical proximity.

Yet Paul does not disappear. Instead, he writes. Letters to Corinth, Ephesus, Philippi, Thessalonica, and others carry instruction, correction, encouragement, and truth across miles and circumstances. Paul leads communities he cannot see daily. He shapes leaders he cannot supervise closely. His influence travels further than his body ever could.

This is not accidental, it is formative. Paul understands that multiplication requires leaders who can lead faithfully without constant oversight. Distance becomes a crucible that reveals whether leadership has truly taken root.

The Leadership Insight

As leaders move into multiplication, proximity inevitably decreases. This is often one of the hardest transitions. Leaders who are relationally strong may feel disoriented when they can no longer be everywhere. They cannot hear every conversation, observe every decision, or correct every misstep in real time. The temptation is either to tighten control through constant communication or to disengage out of fatigue.

Paul models a third way. He guards his influence intentionally. He stays connected without hovering. He speaks clearly without micromanaging. He corrects firmly without shaming. And he trusts leaders to carry responsibility between touchpoints.

Guarded influence is not about controlling outcomes. It is about stewarding clarity. Growth happens in this restraint *so that* leaders learn to trust formation over supervision.

The Guarded Influence Leadership Framework

How leaders lead faithfully when proximity is limited.

Clarify What Matters Most - Anchor on Core Truth
Paul repeatedly returns to essentials, gospel truth, identity in Christ, unity, and holiness. When leaders cannot be present, clarity becomes the guardrail. Leaders must name what is non-negotiable and trust others to apply it.

Clarity protects culture.

Communicate with Intention - Speak with Purpose, Not Volume
Paul's letters are deliberate, not reactive. Guarded influence resists constant communication that creates dependency. Leaders speak thoughtfully, addressing what matters rather than commenting on everything.

Intentional words carry weight.

Correct with Care - Address Issues Without Undermining Leaders
Paul corrects behavior and theology directly, but he does not dismantle leadership publicly. Guarded influence protects dignity while addressing dysfunction.

Correction must preserve trust.

Trust the Work of God - Release Outcomes Beyond Reach
Paul entrusts churches to God's ongoing work. He prays, encourages, and hopes, but he cannot control. Guarded influence recognizes where leadership ends and God's work continues.

Trust completes stewardship.

What This Looks Like at Work

In modern leadership contexts, guarded influence leadership shows up wherever leaders oversee leaders rather than tasks.

In corporate environments, this may look like setting clear expectations and values while allowing leaders to execute locally, measured through outcomes, KPIs, standards, or learning benchmarks without constant oversight. In education or ministry, it may look like equipping leaders with theological and cultural clarity rather than prescribing every response. In trades or operations, it may look like trusting trained leaders to make real-time decisions within safety and quality guardrails.

Guarded influence does not remove accountability. It shifts it. Leaders who attempt to control from a distance often erode trust. Leaders who disengage create drift. Leaders who guard influence well create alignment that holds even when they are not present.

Reflection

- Where does distance in leadership feel most uncomfortable for you?
- How do you currently balance clarity and control when you are not nearby?
- What might need to be clarified so trust can increase?

Scripture to Read

“And now I commend you to God and to the word of his grace, which is able to build you up...”
-Acts 20:32 (ESV)

As you reflect on this verse, what does it look like to entrust people to God rather than to your constant presence?

Invite God Into This

Ask God to help you release anxiety where proximity has decreased.

Invite the Holy Spirit to guide how you communicate, correct, and encourage from a distance. Pray for wisdom to guard influence without controlling outcomes and to trust the work God is doing beyond what you can see.

Leadership is not diminished by distance. It is refined by trust.

Take the Next Step

- **Form a habit:** Clarify one core expectation rather than offering constant direction.
- **Have a conversation:** Ask a leader what clarity would help them lead confidently.
- **Choose a new response:** Reduce unnecessary oversight that creates dependency.

Multiplication requires leaders who can lead without hovering and guarded influence makes that possible.

2 Timothy - Multiplication Mindset Leadership

Faithful people who teach others

The Moment

Paul writes his second letter to Timothy from prison, near the end of his life. There is no pretense of expansion or momentum here. Paul is not strategizing for his next journey. He is not building platforms or protecting reputation, he is preparing for what comes after him.

Timothy is young, pressured, and carrying responsibility in a complex environment. False teaching is spreading. Opposition is growing. Leadership is costly. Paul does not simplify the challenge. He strengthens Timothy's resolve.

Then Paul delivers one of the clearest leadership multiplication statements in all of Scripture.

"What you have heard from me in the presence of many witnesses entrust to faithful men, who will be able to teach others also." (2 Timothy 2:2, ESV)

Four generations of leadership appear in a single sentence:
Paul → Timothy → faithful people → others.

This is not accidental. It is intentional design. Paul understands that leadership multiplication is not about charisma, proximity, or scale. It is about faithful transmission of truth through people who can carry it forward.

The Leadership Insight

Multiplication is not an outcome. It is a mindset. Many leaders measure success by what they personally accomplish. How much they oversee. How many decisions they make. How central they remain to the work. Multiplication challenges all of that.

Paul's instruction to Timothy reframes leadership success entirely. Leadership is not complete when others depend on you. It is complete when others are equipped to lead without you.

This is uncomfortable for many leaders. Multiplication requires patience. It requires relinquishing visibility. It requires trusting others to carry responsibility imperfectly. It requires investing deeply in fewer people rather than managing many at a distance.

Growth happens in this narrowing *so that* leadership expands beyond one generation.

The Multiplication Mindset Leadership Framework

How leaders intentionally design leadership to reproduce.

Entrust Intentionally - Choose Faithfulness Over Flash
Paul does not instruct Timothy to select the most talented or charismatic leaders. He says *faithful*. Multiplication begins with character, not competence alone.

Faithfulness sustains leadership.

Teach Clearly - Pass On What Matters Most
Paul emphasizes what Timothy has *heard*. Multiplication requires clarity. Leaders must know what to pass on and resist overloading others with everything.

Clarity enables reproduction.

Empower Others - Release Responsibility, Not Just Information
Teaching alone is insufficient. Leaders must entrust responsibility. Multiplication accelerates when leaders are trusted to act, decide, and teach others.

Ownership fuels growth.

Think Beyond Yourself - Plan for the Next Generation
Paul's horizon extends beyond his lifetime. Leaders with a multiplication mindset think generationally. They ask not only *Who am I leading now?* but *Who will they lead next?*

Legacy is intentional.

What This Looks Like at Work

In leadership environments today, multiplication mindset leadership shows up when leaders intentionally design systems that develop other leaders.

In corporate settings, this may look like leadership pipelines, mentoring structures, and succession planning, measured through readiness, depth, and consistency rather than just performance metrics, KPIs, or outcomes. In education or ministry, it may look like discipling leaders who can teach, shepherd, and develop others. In trades or operations, it may look like apprenticeship models that prioritize safety, skill, and responsibility transfer.

Multiplication does not happen accidentally. Leaders who fail to plan for reproduction eventually become bottlenecks. Leaders who build for multiplication create movement that continues beyond them.

Reflection

- Who has entrusted leadership to you, and how are you stewarding it?
- Where might you be prioritizing competence over faithfulness?
- Who are you intentionally preparing to lead beyond you?

Scripture to Read

"And what you have heard from me... entrust to faithful men."
-2 Timothy 2:2 (ESV)

As you reflect on this verse, what truth or responsibility might God be asking you to entrust to someone else?

Invite God Into This

Ask God to expand your leadership horizon beyond immediate results.

Invite the Holy Spirit to help you identify faithful people to invest in deeply. Pray for humility to step back when needed and courage to entrust others with meaningful responsibility.

Multiplication is an act of faith.

Take the Next Step

- **Form a habit:** Invest intentionally in one leader's development.
- **Have a conversation:** Ask someone what support would help them grow as a leader.
- **Choose a new response:** Shift from doing to developing in one area of leadership.

Leadership that multiplies does not end with you. It continues through others.

Paul's Finish - Faithful Outcomes Leadership

Steward obedience, release results

The Moment

Paul's final words are not written from a place of victory as the world defines it. He is imprisoned. His influence is limited. Many of his companions have moved on. The future of the churches he planted is uncertain. From the outside, Paul's life could be misread as unfinished or unsuccessful.

But Paul does not frame it that way. Writing to Timothy, Paul reflects on his life with striking clarity.

"I have fought the good fight, I have finished the race, I have kept the faith." (2 Timothy 4:7, ESV)

Paul does not list achievements. He does not measure impact. He does not recount growth metrics or visible wins. He names faithfulness.

Then he looks ahead.

"Henceforth there is laid up for me the crown of righteousness, which the Lord... will award to me on that Day." (2 Timothy 4:8, ESV)

Paul's confidence is not rooted in outcomes he can control. It is rooted in obedience he has already offered.

This is the posture of faithful outcomes leadership.

The Leadership Insight

At some point, every leader must confront a hard truth: outcomes are not fully ours to manage. This becomes especially clear when leaders move into multiplication. As influence expands and proximity decreases, leaders lose the ability to track every decision, measure every impact, or ensure every result. What once felt manageable now feels exposed.

This is where leadership can fracture. Some leaders tighten control, trying to preserve outcomes. Others disengage emotionally, numbing disappointment. Still others tie their identity so tightly to results that they struggle to rest, release, or finish well.

Paul offers a different framework. Faithful leaders steward obedience and entrust outcomes to God.

This does not mean leaders stop caring about results. It means they refuse to let results define their worth, their faithfulness, or their legacy. Paul understands that his role is to run the race assigned to him, not to control how God uses it beyond his lifetime.

Growth happens in this surrender *so that* leaders finish with peace rather than pressure.

The Faithful Outcomes Leadership Framework

How leaders release results while remaining fully faithful.

Run Your Race - Stay Focused on Your Assignment
Paul speaks of *his* race, not everyone else's. Faithful outcomes leadership begins with clarity about calling. Leaders are responsible for obedience to what God has entrusted to them, not comparison to others.

Clarity guards contentment.

Keep the Faith - Measure Faithfulness, Not Applause
Paul defines success as faith kept, not recognition earned. Leaders must regularly recalibrate their metrics, asking whether they are faithful, not just effective.

Faithfulness outlasts performance.

Release the Results - Entrust What Continues Beyond You
Paul knows the work will continue after him. Faithful leaders release control over how God multiplies what they have planted. They trust that obedience is never wasted.

Release completes stewardship.

Finish Well - Leave with Integrity and Hope
Paul's tone is not bitter or anxious. It is confident and hopeful. Leaders who finish well leave behind clarity, trust, and peace, not unresolved tension or unfinished fear.

The finish matters.

What This Looks Like at Work

In leadership environments today, faithful outcomes leadership shows up when leaders resist defining success solely by metrics.

In corporate contexts, this may look like focusing on ethical leadership, sustainability, and development alongside KPIs, outcomes, or benchmarks rather than chasing numbers at the expense of people. In education or ministry, it may look like trusting God with fruit that unfolds over years. In trades or operations, it may look like prioritizing safety, integrity, and craftsmanship even when recognition is delayed.

Faithful outcomes leadership does not abandon measurement. It refuses to worship it.

Leaders who cannot release outcomes often struggle to multiply. Leaders who can release outcomes create space for others to lead freely.

Reflection

- How do you currently define success in your leadership?
- Where might you be holding outcomes more tightly than obedience?
- What would it look like to finish this season of leadership with peace?

Scripture to Read

"So neither he who plants nor he who waters is anything, but only God who gives the growth."
-1 Corinthians 3:7 (ESV)

As you reflect on this verse, what does it mean to trust God with growth you cannot control?

Invite God Into This

Ask God to help you release the outcomes you have been carrying too heavily.

Invite the Holy Spirit to re-anchor your leadership identity in faithfulness rather than results. Pray for grace to finish seasons well, to trust God with what continues beyond you, and to rest in obedience offered fully.

Faithfulness is never wasted.

Take the Next Step

- **Form a habit:** Evaluate decisions through the lens of obedience rather than outcome alone.
- **Have a conversation:** Ask a trusted leader how they define finishing well.
- **Choose a new response:** Release one result you've been trying to control and entrust it to God.

Leadership multiplication does not end with certainty. It ends with trust.

Stage 4 | Lead the Organization - Culture & Systems

Shaping What Outlives You

Leadership eventually reaches a point where proximity is no longer the primary driver of influence. You are no longer shaping everything through direct relationships or daily decisions. Instead, the environment itself begins to lead. Culture teaches. Systems reinforce. Rhythms repeat. Stories get told and retold, sometimes accurately, sometimes not.

This is the moment leadership becomes less about how you show up and more about what you have built.

Stage 4 is about recognizing that leadership at scale is expressed through culture and systems. What gets remembered, what gets rewarded, what gets repeated, and what gets protected begin shaping people more consistently than any single leader can.

Culture is not accidental. It is either intentionally designed or unintentionally inherited.

Scripture consistently reflects this reality. As God's people grow, He establishes practices that preserve identity and purpose. Passover and Communion are not just spiritual moments; they are systems of remembrance. Stones of remembrance are not sentimental gestures; they are organizational memory. Structures in Acts are not bureaucracy; they are protective design. Resistance is not surprising. Pressure is not avoided. Leadership presence, especially under scrutiny, communicates values more powerfully than words ever could.

At this stage, leaders must shift how they understand their responsibility.

- They are no longer primarily responding to problems.
- They are shaping patterns.
- They are aligning mission and motives.
- They are designing systems that support faithfulness rather than erode it.

This is not yet the stage of finishing. It is the stage of **building something that can be finished well.**

Stage 4 focuses on how leaders steward culture and operations so the organization itself supports integrity, alignment, and sustainability.

Stage 4 asks questions like:

- What are we intentionally remembering, and what are we forgetting?
- What behaviors are being reinforced by our systems?
- Where are misalignment and dysfunction actually design problems?
- How do we lead through resistance without reacting out of fear?
- What does composure under pressure teach the people watching us?

This stage is about **infrastructure**, not endurance.

It is about shaping environments that help people do the right thing more often, especially when leaders are not present.

Stage 5 will turn inward again. It will ask how leaders guard their hearts, discern wisely, resist compromise, and remain faithful over time. But **Stage 4** stays outward-facing. Its concern is not whether the leader personally endures, but whether the organization has been shaped to support faithfulness, clarity, and sustainability for everyone within it.

What you build here will either carry people forward or quietly pull them off course.

That's why this stage matters. Because leadership that multiplies leaders must eventually steward systems. And systems, once built, speak long after leaders stop speaking.

Let's build wisely.

Passover & Communion - Remembering Purpose and Identity

Culture is built by what we remember together

The Moment

Before God gives Israel a land, a king, or a military strategy, He gives them a memory. On the night of the Passover, God does more than deliver His people from slavery. He institutes a practice.

“This day shall be for you a memorial day, and you shall keep it as a feast to the LORD… throughout your generations.” (Exodus 12:14, ESV)

Passover is not a one-time event. It is a recurring rhythm. A structured act of remembrance designed to preserve identity long after the moment of rescue has passed.

Later, Jesus does the same. On the night before His crucifixion, He takes bread and a cup and tells His disciples:

“Do this in remembrance of me.” (Luke 22:19, ESV)

Again, this is not a suggestion. It is an instruction. A system of remembrance meant to anchor identity as the movement grows beyond proximity to Jesus Himself.

God does not trust memory to chance. He builds it into the life of His people.

The Leadership Insight

Organizations drift when they forget who they are. Not suddenly. Slowly. As leaders move into organizational leadership, urgency increases. Decisions stack. Problems demand attention. Growth introduces complexity. Over time, the original "why" gets crowded out by the immediate "what now."

This is rarely intentional. But it is predictable. Culture is shaped not only by what leaders say, but by what organizations remember, and what they allow to fade. Without intentional practices of remembrance, purpose erodes, identity blurs, and people begin optimizing for survival instead of mission.

This is why **Stage 4** leadership is not primarily about motivation or charisma. It is about **memory**.

What is remembered together becomes culture. What is forgotten quietly reshapes it.

Growth happens in the discipline of remembrance *so that* organizations stay aligned even as they scale.

The Anchored Identity Framework

How to institutionalize purpose and identity.

Name the Why - Clarify Purpose Explicitly
Passover and Communion both tell a story. Leaders must clearly articulate why the organization exists and what it is called to serve. Vague purpose cannot anchor culture.

Clarity precedes continuity.

Create Shared Rhythms - Build Remembrance into Practice
God does not rely on speeches alone. He establishes rhythms. Leaders at the organizational level must design regular moments, rituals, milestones, reviews, celebrations, that reinforce identity.

Rhythms form culture.

Tell the Story - Repeat It Until It Sticks
In Scripture, remembrance is communal and generational. Leaders must tell the story often enough that people who were not "there at the beginning" still understand who they are part of.

Stories sustain alignment.

Protect the Meaning - Guard Against Drift
Remembrance requires protection. Leaders must notice when symbols lose meaning or rituals become routine. Culture erodes when remembrance becomes mechanical.

Protection preserves purpose.

What This Looks Like at Work

In organizational leadership today, remembering purpose and identity shows up in intentional design choices.

In corporate settings, this may include onboarding that emphasizes mission over metrics, regular reviews that connect outcomes (KPIs, targets, standards, completion rates) back to purpose, and leadership rhythms that reinforce identity beyond performance. In education or ministry, it may include shared practices that remind people why the work matters beyond immediate results. In trades or operations, it may include honoring craftsmanship, safety, and service as expressions of calling, not just compliance.

When organizations fail to remember together, people default to efficiency, urgency, or self-protection.

When organizations remember well, culture stays aligned even under pressure.

Reflection

- What moments or stories currently define your organization's identity?
- What has been remembered intentionally, and what may be fading unintentionally?
- Where might purpose need to be re-anchored through shared practice rather than new language?

Scripture to Read

"Remember the whole way that the LORD your God has led you."
-Deuteronomy 8:2 (ESV)

As you reflect on this passage, what parts of your organization's story need to be remembered more clearly?

Invite God Into This

Ask God to reveal where your organization may be drifting from its original purpose.

Invite the Holy Spirit to guide you in building rhythms that anchor identity and align daily work with calling. Pray for wisdom to remember well (not nostalgically) but faithfully.

Culture is shaped by what we remember together.

Take the Next Step

- **Form a habit:** Identify one existing rhythm that could better reinforce purpose.
- **Have a conversation:** Ask others what they believe your organization exists to do.
- **Choose a new response:** Connect one decision or outcome explicitly back to mission.

Before leaders fix systems, confront resistance, or endure pressure, they must anchor identity. Because organizations that forget who they are eventually lose their way.

Stones of Remembrance - Making Wins Visible

What gets remembered gets repeated

The Moment

When Israel finally crosses the Jordan River into the land God promised, the moment is unmistakably significant. The river stops flowing. The people cross on dry ground. A long season of wandering gives way to arrival.

But before they move forward, God tells Joshua to stop.

"Take twelve men from the people, from each tribe a man, and command them, 'Take twelve stones from here out of the midst of the Jordan... and bring them over with you and lay them down in the place where you lodge tonight.'" (Joshua 4:2–3, ESV)

This is not an efficiency move. It delays momentum.

The stones serve no functional purpose. They do not protect the people, organize the camp, or improve logistics. They exist for one reason only: remembrance.

"When your children ask in time to come, 'What do those stones mean to you?' then you shall tell them..." (Joshua 4:6–7, ESV)

God knows something leaders often forget:

- If wins are not marked, they will be forgotten.
- If they are forgotten, they will not shape culture.

The Leadership Insight

Organizations repeat what they recognize. Leaders often assume that progress speaks for itself. That people will naturally notice what went well. That effort will be remembered because it mattered in the moment. But Scripture tells a different story.

God commands His people to make wins visible *on purpose*.

Not to inflate ego.
Not to create spectacle.
But to preserve meaning.

At the organizational level, what leaders choose to highlight becomes a form of instruction. What is named and remembered teaches people what faithfulness looks like. What goes unmarked quietly communicates that it didn't matter.

This is where culture is either strengthened or diluted.

Growth happens in the intentional marking of meaning *so that* organizations don't drift toward urgency, output, or survival as their primary measure of success.

The Marked Meaning Framework

Reinforce culture through intentional remembrance.

Identify the Win - Name Faithfulness Clearly
Joshua does not assume people will connect the stones to the miracle. Leaders must clearly name *what* is being recognized and *why* it matters. Wins should reflect values, not just results.

Clarity gives meaning.

Make It Visible - Create Shared Markers
The stones are placed where people will see them. Organizational wins should be visible. Shared in meetings, embedded in onboarding, and reflected in rituals or milestones.

Visibility reinforces culture.

Tell the Story - Connect Action to Purpose
The stones prompt storytelling. Leaders must connect wins to purpose so people understand how faithfulness advances the mission.

Stories teach alignment.

Repeat the Pattern - Build Reinforcement into Rhythm
This is not a one-time act. Leaders must create consistent rhythms for recognizing faithfulness so culture is reinforced over time, not occasionally.

Repetition sustains memory.

What This Looks Like at Work

In organizational settings today, making wins visible requires discernment.

In corporate environments, this may include recognizing behaviors that reflect values, not just performance metrics alongside KPIs, targets, standards, or outcomes. In education or ministry, it may include highlighting growth, faithfulness, or service that aligns with purpose rather than spotlighting personalities. In trades or operations, it may include honoring safety, craftsmanship, teamwork, and consistency not just speed or volume.

When wins are only **measured by output**, culture narrows.

When wins are **marked by meaning**, culture deepens.

Leaders who fail to mark wins often wonder why values don't stick. Leaders who mark wins intentionally teach people what success truly looks like.

Reflection

- What kinds of wins are currently visible in your organization?
- What faithfulness might be happening quietly without recognition?
- How does what you celebrate shape what people pursue?

Scripture to Read

"So these stones shall be to the people of Israel a memorial forever." -Joshua 4:7 (ESV)

As you reflect on this verse, what "stones" might your organization need to place?

Invite God Into This

Ask God to help you see where faithfulness is happening that deserves recognition.

Invite the Holy Spirit to guide how you mark wins, not for applause, but for formation. Pray for wisdom to celebrate what aligns with purpose rather than what simply looks impressive.

Culture is shaped by what leaders choose to remember.

Take the Next Step

- **Form a habit:** Notice one behavior that reflects your values and name it publicly.
- **Have a conversation:** Ask someone what wins they think matter most, and why.
- **Choose a new response:** Shift recognition from output alone to alignment with purpose.

Wins don't shape culture when they're achieved. They shape culture when they're remembered.

The Tower of Babel - Aligning Mission and Motives

When success pulls you off course

The Moment

The story of the Tower of Babel is often told as a warning about pride. But at its core, it is a story about alignment or the lack of it. After the flood, humanity is growing. People are organizing, collaborating, and building. On the surface, this looks like progress.

"Then they said, 'Come, let us build ourselves a city and a tower with its top in the heavens, and let us make a name for ourselves...'" (Genesis 11:4, ESV)

The people are unified. They are skilled. They are productive. Their project is ambitious and efficient.

And God intervenes.

This is unsettling for many leaders. Nothing about the project appears chaotic, from the outside, it may not seem wrong or immoral. The issue is not incompetence. The issue is motive.

God had commanded humanity to fill the earth. Babel concentrates power, influence, and identity inward instead. The people are aligned with each other but misaligned with God.

So God disrupts the system.

"Come, let us go down and there confuse their language..." (Genesis 11:7, ESV)

What looks like judgment is actually restraint. God interrupts momentum to prevent misaligned success from becoming entrenched.

The Leadership Insight

Alignment matters more than efficiency. At the organizational level, leaders often mistake unity for faithfulness and momentum for mission. When people are working well together and results are visible, it's tempting to assume the organization is healthy.

But Babel warns leaders that shared effort does not guarantee shared submission. Organizations can be highly functional and deeply misaligned at the same time.

This is why **Stage 4** leadership requires discernment beyond performance. Leaders must regularly ask not just *Are we effective?* but *Are we aligned?* Not just *Is this working?* but *Is this faithful?*

Growth happens in the discomfort of slowed momentum *so that* organizations do not outrun their calling.

The Aligned Direction Framework

Examine alignment beneath visible success.

Clarify the True Aim - Name the "Why" Honestly
The people at Babel name their aim clearly: "Let us make a name for ourselves." Leaders must be willing to name motives honestly, especially when success feels good.

Alignment begins with truth.

Examine Momentum - Don't Let Speed Replace Discernment
Momentum can mask misalignment. Leaders must slow down long enough to examine direction, even when progress feels validating.

Speed is not proof.

Check for Submission - Who Sets the Direction?
At Babel, the people set their own direction. Aligned organizations submit mission and strategy to God rather than assuming autonomy.

Submission anchors leadership.

Interrupt When Necessary - Course-Correct Before Scale
God intervenes early to prevent misaligned systems from scaling. Leaders must be willing to disrupt their own success when alignment is compromised.

Correction protects the future.

What This Looks Like at Work

In organizational leadership today, misalignment often hides behind productivity.

In corporate environments, this may look like growth that prioritizes revenue, KPIs, or output while drifting from purpose, ethics, or people development. In education or ministry, it may look like programs expanding while formation thins. In trades or operations, it may look like speed or volume eclipsing safety, craftsmanship, or care.

Babel reminds leaders that alignment must be examined before systems are reinforced.

Organizations that refuse to question momentum eventually build structures that are hard to undo.

Reflection

- Where is your organization experiencing strong momentum right now?
- What motives might need to be examined beneath that progress?
- How do you currently test alignment beyond results?

Scripture to Read

"Unless the LORD builds the house, those who build it labor in vain."
-Psalm 127:1 (ESV)

As you reflect on this verse, what might God be inviting you to pause or re-align?

Invite God Into This

Ask God to reveal any areas where success may be pulling your organization off course.

Invite the Holy Spirit to refine motives, slow momentum where needed, and realign direction with God's purposes. Pray for courage to interrupt progress if it compromises faithfulness.

Not everything that works is faithful.

Take the Next Step

- **Form a habit:** Ask alignment questions before celebrating results.
- **Have a conversation:** Invite trusted leaders to challenge assumptions about success.
- **Choose a new response:** Pause one initiative long enough to examine its direction.

Organizations don't drift because leaders stop caring. They drift because leaders stop checking alignment.

Acts 6 - Fixing Systems Instead of Blaming People

Protecting the Mission as the Work Multiplies

The Moment

The early church is growing quickly. What began as a close-knit community has expanded into a diverse, multi-cultural movement. With growth comes complexity. And with complexity comes tension.

"Now in these days when the disciples were increasing in number, a complaint by the Hellenists arose against the Hebrews because their widows were being neglected in the daily distribution." (Acts 6:1, ESV)

This is not a theological dispute. It is an operational breakdown. The apostles do not question motives. They do not accuse the church of being unloving. They do not rebuke individuals for negligence. Instead, they recognize something critical: the system that once worked no longer fits the scale of the community.

So they redesign it.

"It is not right that we should give up preaching the word of God to serve tables... pick out from among you seven men... whom we will appoint to this duty." (Acts 6:2–3, ESV)

Roles are clarified. Responsibility is redistributed. A new structure is created.

And the result?

"And the word of God continued to increase, and the number of the disciples multiplied greatly..." (Acts 6:7, ESV)

Growth follows design.

The Leadership Insight

When systems break, leaders often blame people. They assume the issue is effort, attitude, or commitment. They coach harder, remind louder, or pressure more. But Acts 6 offers a different diagnosis.

The problem was not character. It was capacity. The system had not kept pace with the mission.

At the organizational level, blaming people for system failure erodes trust and exhausts leaders. Fixing systems, on the other hand, restores clarity and protects people from carrying weight they were never meant to hold.

Growth happens when leaders shift from personal blame to structural responsibility *so that* organizations can scale without sacrificing care.

The Redemptive Design Framework

Respond to breakdowns with wisdom rather than accusation.

Diagnose the Breakdown - Look Beneath Behavior
The apostles notice a pattern, not a personality. Leaders must ask whether dysfunction is truly about people, or about design that no longer fits reality.

Patterns reveal system strain.

Clarify Roles - Assign Responsibility Intentionally
Acts 6 establishes clear ownership. Leaders protect the mission by ensuring responsibilities are distributed according to calling and capacity.

Clarity reduces friction.

Redesign the Process - Adjust for Scale
The solution is not more effort, but better structure. Leaders must be willing to change systems that once worked but no longer serve the organization well.

Design enables sustainability.

Protect the Mission - Keep the Main Thing Central
The apostles refuse to abandon their primary calling. Healthy systems free leaders to focus on what only they can do.

Structure serves purpose.

What This Looks Like at Work

In organizational leadership today, system breakdowns often show up as people problems.

In corporate environments, this may look like missed deadlines, burnout, or inconsistent performance measured through KPIs, outcomes, or targets when the real issue is unclear ownership or overloaded processes. In education or ministry, it may look like leaders stretched thin because roles were never clarified. In trades or operations, it may look like safety lapses caused by rushed workflows rather than negligence.

Blame creates fear. Design creates freedom. Organizations that refuse to fix systems eventually lose good people. Organizations that redesign wisely protect both mission and morale.

Reflection

- Where might people be carrying responsibility your systems were never designed to support?
- What recurring issues suggest a design problem rather than a motivation problem?
- How do you typically respond when something breaks down by coaching people or examining structure?

Scripture to Read

"Let all things be done decently and in order."
-1 Corinthians 14:40 (ESV)

As you reflect on this verse, where might order bring relief rather than restriction?

Invite God Into This

Ask God for wisdom to see design problems clearly.

Invite the Holy Spirit to help you release blame and pursue redemptive solutions that protect people and advance the mission. Pray for courage to change systems, even ones you helped build.

Good design is an act of love.

Take the Next Step

- **Form a habit:** When an issue repeats, ask what system might be contributing.
- **Have a conversation:** Invite feedback about where processes feel strained.
- **Choose a new response:** Redesign one small workflow instead of correcting behavior.

Organizations don't break because people stop caring. They break because systems stop serving.

Nehemiah - Leading Through Resistance

Steady leadership when pushback comes

The Moment

Nehemiah's leadership is often remembered for vision and execution. But the longer story reveals something else just as important: resistance is constant.

As soon as rebuilding begins, opposition shows up.

"But when Sanballat and Tobiah and the Arabs and the Ammonites and the Ashdodites heard that the repairing of the walls of Jerusalem was going forward... they were very angry." (Nehemiah 4:7, ESV)

The resistance is layered. It starts with mockery. Then intimidation. Then threats and then internal fatigue and discouragement. The work itself becomes harder, and the voices questioning whether it's worth continuing grow louder.

What's striking is that Nehemiah does not interpret resistance as a sign to stop. He treats it as part of the work.

“So we prayed to our God and set a guard as a protection against them day and night.” (Nehemiah 4:9, ESV)

Prayer and planning. Trust and structure. Faith and strategy working together.

The Leadership Insight

Resistance often increases when leaders are doing the right work. At the organizational level, change disrupts comfort. Systems are being altered. Power is being redistributed. Old patterns are challenged. People who benefited from the previous environment may push back-not always maliciously, but predictably.

This is where leaders can misread the moment. Some interpret resistance as failure and retreat prematurely. Others react defensively, escalating conflict and eroding trust. Nehemiah models a third way.

He remains steady. He does not deny the resistance, and he does not become consumed by it. He acknowledges the threat, strengthens the people, and keeps building.

Growth happens in this steadiness *so that* leaders do not abandon necessary work simply because it becomes difficult.

The Steady Resistance Framework

Respond to resistance without overreacting or withdrawing.

Expect Resistance - Normalize Pushback
Nehemiah is not surprised. Leaders who expect resistance are less likely to personalize it. Change always surfaces discomfort.

Expectation reduces panic.

Discern the Source - Separate Fear from Sabotage
Not all resistance is the same. Some comes from fear and fatigue. Some comes from threatened interests. Leaders must discern rather than assume intent.

Discernment shapes response.

Strengthen the People - Reinforce Purpose and Capability
Nehemiah reminds the people why the work matters.

"Remember the Lord, who is great and awesome..." (Nehemiah 4:14, ESV)

Leaders strengthen resolve by reconnecting people to purpose. Purpose fuels perseverance.

Protect the Work - Put Guardrails in Place
Nehemiah adjusts the system. Some build while others stand guard. He adapts the structure to meet the moment.

Protection enables progress.

What This Looks Like at Work

In organizational leadership today, resistance often surfaces when systems change. In corporate settings, this may look like pushback when roles, processes, or accountability structures are clarified. In education or ministry, it may look like discomfort when long-standing habits are challenged. In trades or operations, it may look like resistance to new safety standards or workflows.

Leaders must resist the temptation to either placate resistance or crush it.

- Steady leadership listens, discerns, and continues building.
- Organizations stall when leaders mistake resistance for rebellion.
- Organizations fracture when leaders respond with fear or force.
- Organizations grow when leaders stay steady and adaptive.

Reflection

- Where are you encountering resistance right now?
- What type of resistance might it be, fear, fatigue, or threatened control?
- How does your response shape the culture during change?

Scripture to Read

"Do not be afraid of them. Remember the Lord..."
-Nehemiah 4:14 (ESV)

As you reflect on this verse, how might remembering God's presence change your response to resistance?

Invite God Into This

Ask God for discernment to understand resistance clearly.

Invite the Holy Spirit to steady your leadership, helping you respond without fear, reactiveness, or retreat. Pray for wisdom to protect the work while caring for the people involved.

Resistance does not mean stop. It means lead steadily.

Take the Next Step

- **Form a habit:** Pause before reacting to resistance and assess its source.
- **Have a conversation:** Ask someone what concerns or fears might be driving pushback.
- **Choose a new response:** Adjust a system or structure to protect progress during change.

Leaders who remain steady under resistance build cultures that can change without breaking.

Jesus Before Pilate - Composure Under Pressure

When presence speaks louder than power

The Moment

Jesus stands before Pilate with everything at stake. He has been falsely accused. The crowd is hostile. Political pressure is mounting. Pilate holds legal authority, public influence, and the power to release or condemn Him.

And yet, Jesus does not rush to defend Himself.

"But Jesus made no further answer, *so that* Pilate was amazed." (Mark 15:5, ESV)

This is not weakness. This is restraint.

Jesus is not passive. He is composed. He speaks when clarity is needed and remains silent when words would serve no purpose. He refuses to be pulled into panic, performance, or posturing.

Pilate, the one with formal authority, is the one unsettled. The one without positional power carries the room.

The Leadership Insight

At the organizational level, leaders are always being watched. Not just when things are going well, but especially when they are not.

Pressure reveals formation. Under scrutiny, leaders teach people what truly matters by how they respond. Composure is not about suppressing emotion; it is about choosing presence over reaction.

Many leaders underestimate this. They assume culture is shaped primarily by policies, systems, and strategy. But when pressure rises, people look to leadership behavior for cues. Tone becomes instruction. Pace becomes permission. Anxiety becomes contagious.

Jesus shows us something countercultural.

Authority does not require noise.
Confidence does not require control.
Leadership does not require constant explanation.

Growth happens in restraint *so that* leaders do not unintentionally teach fear, defensiveness, or instability.

The Centered Authority Framework

Model stability when pressure is high.

Stay Grounded - Anchor Before Responding

Jesus does not react impulsively. Leaders who stay grounded, both emotionally and spiritually, create stability for others. Presence begins with inner anchoring.

Grounding precedes clarity.

Choose Silence Wisely - Speak Only What Serves

Jesus speaks when necessary and remains silent when words would escalate. Leaders must discern when explanation helps and when it distracts.

Silence can be leadership.

Hold the Room - Regulate Tone and Pace

Composure shapes atmosphere. Leaders who slow down, steady their voice, and regulate emotion help others stay regulated as well.

Regulation creates trust.

Release Control - Refuse the Need to Win

Jesus does not attempt to control the outcome. Leaders who release the need to win every moment preserve credibility and integrity.

Authority is not force.

What This Looks Like at Work

In organizational leadership today, composure under pressure is tested constantly. In corporate settings, this may show up during performance challenges, public scrutiny, or high-stakes decisions tied to KPIs, outcomes, or targets. In education or ministry, it may surface during conflict, criticism, or moments of public tension. In trades or operations, it may appear when safety incidents, deadlines, or failures occur.

Leaders who react emotionally amplify stress. Leaders who remain composed create space for problem-solving and trust.

Composure does not mean indifference. It means intentional leadership presence.

Reflection

- How do you typically respond when pressure is high?
- What does your tone teach others in tense moments?
- Where might silence serve leadership better than explanation?

Scripture to Read

"When he was reviled, he did not revile in return."
-1 Peter 2:23 (ESV)

As you reflect on this verse, what does restraint look like in your leadership context?

Invite God Into This

Ask God to anchor you when pressure rises.

Invite the Holy Spirit to help you lead from composure rather than control, from presence rather than panic. Pray for wisdom to know when to speak and when silence serves the moment best.

Leadership presence forms culture.

Take the Next Step

- **Form a habit:** Pause before responding in high-pressure moments.
- **Have a conversation:** Ask trusted leaders how your presence impacts them under stress.
- **Choose a new response:** Slow your pace and tone intentionally during tense situations.

When leaders stay centered under pressure, organizations learn how to remain steady too.

Final Charge - Stewarding Culture So It Outlives You

Building environments that carry faithfulness forward

The Moment

As Moses prepares to die, he does something that feels unexpected. He does not introduce new initiatives. He does not expand the mission. He does not chase momentum. Instead, he gathers the people and reminds them, again, of who God is, who they are, and how they are to live once he is gone.

“Take to heart all the words by which I am warning you today... that you may command them to your children.” (Deuteronomy 32:46, ESV)

Moses knows something leaders at scale must learn. When leadership transitions from presence to absence, what remains is not personality but structure, memory, and practice. The future faithfulness of the people will depend less on Moses himself and more on what has been embedded into the life of the community. This is stewardship at the organizational level.

The Leadership Insight

Leaders do not own culture. They steward it. By the time leaders reach this stage, they have already shaped far more than they realize. Decisions have accumulated. Systems have normalized behavior. Stories have been reinforced. Defaults have been established.

The question is no longer What am I leading? It is What have I built?

Stage 4 leadership requires leaders to take responsibility for the environments they've shaped without defensiveness and without ego. Stewardship means recognizing that culture will continue forming people long after leaders step back from daily influence.

This is not about legacy in the personal sense. That belongs to the next stage. This is about organizational faithfulness. Growth happens when leaders accept stewardship *so that* culture becomes an ally rather than an obstacle to mission.

The Enduring Stewardship Framework

Evaluate and steward what will endure beyond their presence.

Examine What's Embedded - Identify Cultural Defaults
Stewardship begins with honesty. Leaders must assess what happens by default when no one intervenes. Those defaults reveal the true culture.

Defaults reveal design.

Strengthen What Serves - Reinforce Faithful Patterns
Not everything needs to change. Leaders should intentionally strengthen systems, rhythms, and behaviors that support alignment and faithfulness.

Reinforcement stabilizes culture.

Address What Undermines - Correct with Care
Stewardship includes correction. Leaders must name misalignment without blame and adjust systems that quietly erode trust, clarity, or integrity.

Correction protects the future.

Prepare for Continuity - Build Beyond Individuals
Healthy organizations do not depend on irreplaceable leaders. They depend on clear purpose, shared practices, and systems that support consistent leadership.

Continuity sustains mission.

What This Looks Like at Work

In organizational leadership today, stewarding culture requires intentional design.

In corporate environments, this may include ensuring that incentives, metrics (KPIs, outcomes, standards, completion measures), and promotion criteria reinforce stated values. In education or ministry, it may include embedding purpose into rhythms, governance, and leadership development. In trades or operations, it may include designing systems that protect safety, craftsmanship, and people, not just output.

Organizations drift when culture is left unattended and they mature when culture is stewarded deliberately.

Leaders who ignore stewardship leave behind confusion. Leaders who practice it leave behind clarity.

Reflection

- What aspects of your organization will continue shaping people without your involvement?
- Which systems or rhythms most clearly reflect your mission, and which quietly undermine it?
- What responsibility do you need to own rather than delegate away?

Scripture to Read

“Moreover, it is required of stewards that they be found faithful.”
-1 Corinthians 4:2 (ESV)

As you reflect on this verse, what does faithfulness look like at the organizational level right now?

Invite God Into This

Ask God for wisdom to steward what has been built.

Invite the Holy Spirit to help you see culture clearly, what is strong, what is fragile, and what needs care. Pray for humility to correct misalignment and courage to reinforce what honors God.

Stewardship is an act of love for people you may never lead directly.

Take the Next Step

- **Form a habit:** Regularly evaluate what your systems are teaching people.
- **Have a conversation:** Ask leaders what feels most formative in your organization.
- **Choose a new response:** Strengthen one system that supports faithfulness.

Culture does not outlive leaders by accident. It endures because someone chose to steward it.

Turning the Page: From Building to Becoming

Leadership does not move in straight lines. It moves in seasons.

Stage 1 focused on leading yourself, taking responsibility for your character, habits, and inner life. It established that leadership formation always starts internally, long before it becomes visible. Lessons worth returning to regularly, because growth in character is never finished.

Stage 2 shifted the focus outward to leading teams with presence, trust, and relational wisdom. You were reminded that people are not problems to solve, but lives to steward. Relationships require continual attention, and the principles of healthy leadership are practices to revisit, not achievements to outgrow.

Stage 3 asked more of you. Leadership from proximity to multiplication. You explored how to lead leaders, release control, entrust responsibility, and trust God with outcomes you could no longer manage personally. Multiplication isn't a destination, but a continual act of faith.

Stage 4 expanded leadership beyond people and into environments. You considered how culture is formed, how systems disciple, how alignment matters more than momentum, and how composure under pressure becomes organizational instruction. You began shaping what outlives you.

- Each stage required growth.
- Each stage introduced new responsibility.
- And now, leadership shifts one final time.

Not outward but inward again.

Stage 5 | Lead for Legacy - Faithfulness Over Time

Finishing well

The final stage of leadership is not about expansion. It is about endurance.

Scripture is clear and sobering on this point. Many leaders did not fail at the beginning. They drifted later. Slowly. Quietly. Through distraction, compromise, fatigue, misplaced trust, or unchecked patterns that went unexamined for too long.

Stage 5 does not introduce new leadership skills. It introduces **guardrails**.

This stage asks a different set of questions:

Not How do I grow?
Not How do I build?
But How do I remain faithful?

This is the stage where leadership becomes deeply personal again, but not in the way it was at the beginning. Early leadership is shaped by learning.

Late leadership is shaped by vigilance.

> Discernment matters more than drive.
> Humility matters more than influence.
> Integrity matters more than opportunity.
> Daily dependence matters more than momentum.

Stage 5 addresses the spiritual and ethical realities leaders face over time, the slow erosion that can happen when success accumulates, when familiarity dulls wisdom, or when pressure clouds discernment. This stage will explore:

- Guarding against compromise before it becomes collapse,
- Filtering voices and counsel with wisdom,
- Releasing what no longer serves faithfulness,
- Facing failure honestly rather than defensively,
- Staying focused when distraction is subtle,
- Maintaining rhythms of dependence that sustain the soul.

This stage is not about fear; it is about clarity.

It is not about perfection; it is about faithfulness.

Stage 5 does not ask you to retreat from leadership. It asks you to lead with greater awareness of your limits, your vulnerabilities, and your need for God's sustaining presence.

Because leadership is not finished when influence peaks. It is finished when faith is kept.

Eve & Rehoboam - Filtering Voices and Counsel

Faithfulness depends on who you listen to

The Moment

Earlier in this book, we spent time with Eve in the garden. At that point, the focus was foundational, how temptation enters, how truth is questioned, how early leadership formation begins with trust and obedience. Eve helped us see how leadership always starts internally, long before it becomes visible or influential.

Now, we return to her story from a different angle. This time, the question is not What is temptation? to Which voices are shaping direction over time?

In the garden, Eve is not isolated, angry, or defiant. She is engaged in conversation. The serpent does not deny God outright. He reframes Him.

"Did God actually say...?" (Genesis 3:1, ESV)

The question sounds curious. Reasonable. Even thoughtful. But it introduces doubt by subtly repositioning authority. God's words are no longer the fixed reference point. They become negotiable.

Later in Scripture, Rehoboam makes a remarkably similar mistake. When he becomes king, the people ask him to lighten the burden his father placed on them. Rehoboam seeks counsel first from the elders who served Solomon, then from his peers.

"But he abandoned the counsel of the old men… and took counsel with the young men who had grown up with him." (1 Kings 12:8, ESV)

The issue is not that Rehoboam refuses counsel. It's that he chooses voices that affirm what he already wants to do.

Both Eve and Rehoboam listen.
Both make decisions.
Both experience devastating consequences.

The drift begins not with action but with influence.

The Leadership Insight

Leaders rarely drift because they stop listening. They drift because they stop **filtering**.

At this stage of leadership, voices multiply. Influence expands. Feedback comes faster and louder from peers, platforms, advisors, critics, and well-meaning supporters. Not all of it is wrong. Not all of it is wise.

Stage 5 leadership requires a sober realization:

Every voice carries a bias.
Every counsel reflects a lens.
Every influence shapes direction.

Faithfulness over time depends less on access to counsel and more on discernment about which voices carry weight.

Growth happens in the discipline of filtering *so that* leaders do not confuse affirmation with wisdom or familiarity with truth.

The Discerned Voices Framework

Steward influence without surrendering authority.

Name the Source - Identify Where the Voice Is Rooted
The serpent reframes God's word. Rehoboam's peers reflect his insecurities. Leaders must ask: *Where is this voice coming from?* Experience, fear, ambition, faithfulness, or convenience?

Source determines credibility.

Weigh the Fruit - Examine the Likely Outcome
Scripture consistently evaluates counsel by its fruit. Leaders must consider what a voice produces over time, not just how it sounds in the moment.

Fruit reveals wisdom.

Check for Alignment - Measure Against God's Word
Eve's error begins when God's instruction is no longer the anchor. Leaders must hold every voice (internal and external) against Scripture.

Alignment protects authority.

Choose Intentionally - Decide Who Shapes You
Rehoboam chooses his counselors. Leaders always do. Faithfulness requires intentional selection, not passive absorption.

Choice sustains discernment.

What This Looks Like at Work

In leadership today, filtering voices is increasingly difficult.

In corporate environments, leaders are surrounded by metrics, opinions, dashboards, KPIs, outcomes, and constant feedback loops. In ministry and education, leaders face congregational pressure, cultural commentary, and spiritualized opinions. In trades and operations, leaders hear urgency, speed, and efficiency competing with safety, craftsmanship, and care.

Not every voice deserves the same weight.

Leaders who fail to filter counsel often call it collaboration until the drift becomes visible.

Leaders who filter wisely protect clarity without isolating themselves.

Reflection

- Whose voices currently influence your decisions the most?
- Which voices affirm your instincts, and which challenge them? Which voices confirm what the Holy Spirit is telling you?
- Where might familiarity be replacing discernment?

Scripture to Read

"The way of a fool is right in his own eyes, but a wise man listens to advice."
-Proverbs 12:15 (ESV)

As you reflect on this verse, how do you distinguish wise counsel from convenient agreement?

Invite God Into This

Ask God to sharpen your discernment.

Invite the Holy Spirit to reveal which voices deserve weight and which need boundaries. Pray for humility to listen well and courage to filter wisely.

Faithfulness begins with discernment.

Take the Next Step

- **Form a habit:** Pause before acting on advice, especially advice that feels affirming.
- **Have a conversation:** Ask a trusted, grounded voice to challenge your thinking.
- **Choose a new response:** Limit exposure to voices that create confusion rather than clarity.

Leadership rarely fails loudly. It drifts quietly, one voice at a time.

Samson & Ahab - Guarding Against Compromise

Drift rarely starts where it ends

The Moment

Samson and Ahab could not look more different on the surface. Samson is physically powerful, called from birth, set apart by God with visible signs of divine favor. Ahab is politically powerful, positioned as king, surrounded by resources, authority, and influence.

Yet their stories converge in the same place. Compromise.

Samson's calling is clear. His boundaries are explicit. His strength is undeniable. But his story is marked by a slow erosion of restraint each choice nudging him closer to the edge.

"She pressed him hard with her words day after day, and urged him, and his soul was vexed to death." (Judges 16:16, ESV)

Nothing collapses all at once. Samson crosses lines gradually, until the line that mattered most no longer feels significant.

Ahab's drift is quieter but just as destructive.

"And Ahab did more to provoke the LORD, the God of Israel, to anger than all the kings of Israel who were before him." (1 Kings 16:33, ESV)

Ahab repeatedly defers responsibility, tolerates evil, and allows influence, especially Jezebel's, to shape decisions he was meant to steward. His failure is not ignorance. It is accommodation.

Both leaders lose clarity long before they lose position.

The Leadership Insight

Leaders rarely wake up one day and decide to abandon faithfulness. They allow small compromises to stack.

Stage 5 leadership recognizes that long-term failure is often the result of short-term tolerance.

What leaders excuse today becomes what defines them tomorrow.

This is especially dangerous for experienced leaders. Success builds confidence. Familiarity dulls urgency. Over time, boundaries that once felt essential start to feel inconvenient.

Growth happens when leaders name compromise early *so that* faithfulness does not erode quietly.

The Guarded Integrity Framework

Identify and address compromise before it becomes collapse.

Notice the Drift - Pay Attention to Small Shifts
Samson doesn't lose strength in one moment. Ahab doesn't reject God outright. Leaders must notice where they are slowly accommodating what once required resistance.

Drift precedes downfall.

Name the Cost - Stop Minimizing Consequences
Both leaders underestimate the cost of compromise. Leaders must honestly name what is at stake, not just personally, but organizationally and spiritually.

Minimization fuels erosion.

Reinforce Boundaries - Recommit to What Protects You
Boundaries are not limitations; they are protection. Leaders must revisit and reinforce guardrails as influence grows.

Protection sustains calling.

Invite Accountability - Don't Guard Integrity Alone
Neither Samson nor Ahab welcomes corrective voices. Leaders who endure invite accountability before it is forced upon them.

Community strengthens integrity.

What This Looks Like at Work

In leadership today, compromise often hides behind rationalization.

In corporate settings, it may look like bending ethical standards to hit targets, KPIs, or outcomes. In ministry or education, it may look like tolerating behavior that contradicts values because confrontation feels costly. In trades or operations, it may look like cutting safety corners for speed or convenience.

Compromise is rarely framed as rebellion. It is framed as practicality.

Leaders who guard integrity must resist the urge to justify what erodes trust over time.

Reflection

- Where might small compromises be stacking in your leadership?
- What boundaries have become easier to ignore as familiarity has grown?
- Who has permission to challenge you when drift begins?

Scripture to Read

"Whoever is faithful in a very little is faithful also in much."
-Luke 16:10 (ESV)

As you reflect on this verse, what "small" areas deserve renewed attention?

Invite God Into This

Ask God to reveal any areas where compromise has been normalized.

Invite the Holy Spirit to strengthen your resolve, restore clarity, and reinforce the guardrails that protect faithfulness. Pray for courage to address drift before it becomes visible failure.

Faithfulness is preserved through vigilance.

Take the Next Step

- **Form a habit:** Name one boundary that needs reinforcement.
- **Have a conversation:** Invite accountability around a known pressure point.
- **Choose a new response:** Stop rationalizing one small compromise.

Leaders do not fall suddenly. They drift until someone chooses to stop.

Lot's Wife - Letting Go of the Past

What you cling to can pull you back

The Moment

Lot's wife is remembered for a single action. As God rescues Lot and his family from the destruction of Sodom, the instructions are clear.

"Escape for your life. Do not look back or stop anywhere in the valley." (Genesis 19:17, ESV)

The command is not arbitrary. It is protective. Yet as the city is judged and the family flees, Lot's wife looks back.

"But Lot's wife, behind him, looked back, and she became a pillar of salt." (Genesis 19:26, ESV)

Scripture gives no explanation for her glance. No motive. No justification. And that silence matters.

Because looking back is rarely about curiosity alone. It often signals attachment, whether it is grief, longing, unresolved identity, or a heart still tethered to what God has already declared unlivable.

The Leadership Insight

Leaders do not drift only because of temptation or compromise. Sometimes they drift because they cannot let go.

At this stage of leadership, the danger is not always overt sin or poor judgment. It is nostalgia. Familiar success. Old identities. Former seasons that once made sense but no longer fit where God is leading.

Lot's wife is not warned about running toward sin. She is warned about looking backward.

Growth happens when leaders release what God has already called them out of *so that* faithfulness is not compromised by attachment to the past.

The Released Attachment Framework

Discern when attachment is hindering obedience.

Recognize Attachment - Notice What Still Has a Hold
The look backward reveals unresolved attachment. Leaders must ask what past seasons, roles, successes, or identities still exert emotional pull.

Attachment reveals allegiance.

Name the Cost - Acknowledge the Risk of Holding On
Looking back carries consequence. Leaders must honestly assess how clinging to the past affects present obedience and future faithfulness.

Clinging distorts direction.

Release Intentionally - Choose Obedience Over Familiarity
Letting go is not passive. It is a decision. Leaders must actively release what God has clearly called them beyond.

Release enables movement.

Reorient Forward - Fix Your Eyes on Where God Is Leading
Faithfulness requires forward focus. Leaders must continually reorient toward God's direction rather than past comfort.

Focus sustains obedience.

What This Looks Like at Work

In leadership today, attachment often hides behind sentimentality.

In corporate environments, leaders may cling to outdated strategies, structures, or successes that no longer serve the organization. In ministry or education, leaders may hold tightly to past models or seasons that once worked but now limit growth. In trades or operations, leaders may resist change because "this is how we've always done it."

Not every past season is meant to be revisited. Some are meant to be honored and then released.

Leaders who refuse to let go often confuse loyalty with obedience.

Reflection

- What past season, role, or identity still has emotional weight for you?
- Where might nostalgia be influencing your leadership decisions?
- What might God be asking you to release in order to move forward faithfully?

Scripture to Read

"Forgetting what lies behind and straining forward to what lies ahead."
-Philippians 3:13 (ESV)

As you reflect on this verse, what does faithful forward movement look like right now?

Invite God Into This

Ask God to reveal any attachments that hinder obedience.

Invite the Holy Spirit to help you release what no longer serves faithfulness and to trust God with what has been left behind. Pray for courage to move forward without turning back.

Faithfulness often requires release.

Take the Next Step

- **Form a habit:** Notice when past success influences present decisions.
- **Have a conversation:** Talk with a trusted leader about what may need to be released.
- **Choose a new response:** Stop referencing the past as justification for current resistance.

God's rescue always leads somewhere. Faithfulness requires following without looking back.

Jonah, Peter, and David - Facing Failure Honestly

Faithfulness is revealed by what you do after you fall

The Moment

Jonah runs. Peter denies. David sins.

These are not minor missteps. They are public, consequential failures by leaders who knew God, heard His voice, and carried real responsibility.

Jonah flees from God's call and boards a ship in the opposite direction.

"But Jonah rose to flee to Tarshish from the presence of the LORD." (Jonah 1:3, ESV)

Peter, under pressure, denies Jesus three times just hours after pledging loyalty.

"Then he began to invoke a curse on himself and to swear, 'I do not know the man.'" (Matthew 26:74, ESV)

David abuses power, commits adultery, orchestrates deception, and causes irreparable harm.

“Why have you despised the word of the LORD, to do what is evil in his sight?” (2 Samuel 12:9, ESV)

What unites these men is not the failure itself. It is what happens next. Jonah resists repentance until he cannot avoid it. Peter weeps bitterly and later receives restoration. David confesses fully and lives with the consequences of his sin.

Scripture does not sanitize their stories. And it does not end them either.

The Leadership Insight

Failure is inevitable in long-term leadership. What is not inevitable is how leaders respond to it.

At this stage, failure becomes especially dangerous, not because it is larger, but because leaders are more skilled at hiding, justifying, or reframing it. Experience can dull urgency. Position can buffer consequence.

Stage 5 leadership requires a defining choice: Will failure become a teacher or a fracture?

Growth happens when leaders face failure honestly *so that* repentance, restoration, and humility remain possible.

The Restored Leadership Framework

Move through failure with integrity rather than avoidance.

Acknowledge the Failure - Stop Minimizing or Deflecting
David names his sin. Peter weeps openly. Leaders must resist defensiveness and speak truthfully about what occurred.

Honesty opens restoration.

Accept the Consequences - Don't Demand Erasure
David's forgiveness does not erase consequence. Leaders must accept what remains without resentment.

Humility sustains credibility.

Receive Restoration - Don't Self-Disqualify
Peter is restored by Jesus, not by his own effort. Leaders must receive grace rather than punishing themselves indefinitely.

Grace reassigns purpose.

Live Changed - Let Repentance Shape the Future
Restoration is not a reset. It is a reformation. Leaders live differently because they have been corrected.

Transformation proves sincerity.

What This Looks Like at Work

In leadership today, failure is often managed rather than faced.

In corporate environments, leaders may spin outcomes, shift blame, or quietly move on without reflection especially when metrics, KPIs, or targets are at stake. In ministry or education, leaders may spiritualize failure or hide behind language of calling. In trades or operations, leaders may downplay mistakes to preserve authority.

But unaddressed failure corrodes trust. Leaders who face failure honestly model humility, accountability, and resilience for those watching.

Reflection

- How do you typically respond when you fail?
- Where might you be minimizing, justifying, or avoiding accountability?
- What would honest repentance look like in your current season?

Scripture to Read

"Create in me a clean heart, O God."
-Psalm 51:10 (ESV)

As you reflect on this verse, what needs to be brought fully into the light?

Invite God Into This

Ask God for courage to face failure honestly.

Invite the Holy Spirit to convict without condemning, to restore without excusing, and to reshape your leadership through repentance. Pray for humility to receive both grace and correction.

Faithfulness is not the absence of failure. It is the willingness to respond truthfully when failure occurs.

Take the Next Step

- **Form a habit:** Reflect honestly after mistakes rather than rushing forward.
- **Have a conversation:** Confess a failure to a trusted, mature believer.
- **Choose a new response:** Stop protecting your image and start protecting your integrity.

God redeems honest failure. He resists hidden pride.

Peter on the Water - Staying Focused Under Pressure

What you fix your eyes on shapes where you stand

The Moment

Peter steps out of the boat. That alone is remarkable.

When Jesus comes to the disciples walking on the water, Peter does not hesitate to ask for permission.

"Lord, if it is you, command me to come to you on the water." (Matthew 14:28, ESV)

Jesus invites him. Peter steps onto the surface and does the impossible, he walks toward Jesus. But then something shifts.

"But when he saw the wind, he was afraid, and beginning to sink he cried out, 'Lord, save me.'" (Matthew 14:30, ESV)

Peter does not sink because he doubts Jesus exists, he sinks because his focus shifts. The wind was there the whole time. The waves had not changed. What changed was what held his attention.

The Leadership Insight

Pressure does not always break leaders through opposition. Sometimes it breaks them through distraction.

At this stage of leadership, pressure is familiar. Expectations are constant. Stakes are high. Leaders learn to function amid noise, urgency, and competing demands. Over time, the danger is not fear, it is divided focus.

Peter's failure is instructive.

He is not rebuked for stepping out.
He is not condemned for fear.
He is corrected for where he placed his attention.

"O you of little faith, why did you doubt?" (Matthew 14:31, ESV)

Faithfulness over time requires leaders to guard focus deliberately. Not every pressure deserves attention. Not every wave deserves analysis.

Growth happens when leaders discipline attention *so that* trust remains centered on Christ rather than circumstances.

The Fixed Focus Framework

Remain anchored when pressure intensifies.

Fix on the Call - Remember Why You Stepped Out
Peter responds to Jesus' invitation. Leaders must continually recall the call that initiated obedience, especially when conditions become uncomfortable.

Calling steadies courage.

Acknowledge the Wind - Don't Deny Reality
Jesus does not deny the storm. Leaders do not need to pretend pressure is absent. Faithful focus acknowledges reality without surrendering attention to it.

Awareness prevents denial.

Refuse the Spiral - Interrupt Fear Early
Peter begins to sink only after fear takes hold. Leaders must notice when attention starts spiraling toward threat rather than trust.

Early correction matters.

Reach for Help - Depend Rather Than Perform
Peter cries out to Jesus. Leaders who endure do not power through alone. They reach for help quickly.

Dependence restores stability.

What This Looks Like at Work

In leadership today, pressure often fragments focus.

In corporate settings, leaders are pulled between metrics, KPIs, outcomes, stakeholder expectations, and constant decision-making. In ministry or education, leaders carry emotional weight, criticism, and the needs of others. In trades or operations, leaders manage safety risks, timelines, and unpredictability.

The wind is always present. Leaders who remain focused do not eliminate pressure, they choose where to look.

Attention becomes a spiritual discipline.

Reflection

- What currently competes for your attention when pressure rises?
- Where does fear begin to redirect your focus?
- What helps you re-center when distraction sets in?

Scripture to Read

"Let us run with endurance the race that is set before us, looking to Jesus."
-Hebrews 12:1–2 (ESV)

As you reflect on this passage, what would it look like to fix your gaze more intentionally?

Invite God Into This

Ask God to steady your focus.

Invite the Holy Spirit to help you notice when attention drifts toward fear, pressure, or performance. Pray for grace to re-center quickly and trust deeply.

Focus is a form of faithfulness.

Take the Next Step

- **Form a habit:** Notice where your attention goes under stress.
- **Have a conversation:** Share pressure honestly rather than carrying it alone.
- **Choose a new response:** Create one intentional pause to re-center during your day.

Leaders don't sink because the storm is strong. They sink when their focus shifts.

Sabbath, Manna, and Prayer - Daily Dependence Over Time

Faithfulness is sustained one day at a time

The Moment

God teaches His people dependence before He ever teaches them endurance. In the wilderness, Israel receives manna as a daily provision with daily limits.

“Gather of it, each one of you, as much as he can eat... But they did not listen to Moses. Some left part of it till the morning, and it bred worms and stank.” (Exodus 16:16, 20, ESV)

Yesterday’s manna cannot be stored for today. Trust must be renewed daily. Alongside manna, God establishes Sabbath.

“Six days you shall labor, but on the seventh day you shall rest.” (Exodus 34:21, ESV)

Rest is not a reward for faithfulness. It is a requirement for it.

And throughout Scripture, prayer is the steady undercurrent, leaders returning again and again to God, not just in crisis, but in ordinary dependence.

Jesus Himself models this rhythm.

"And rising very early in the morning, while it was still dark, he departed and went out to a desolate place, and there he prayed." (Mark 1:35, ESV)

Daily dependence is not a concession to weakness. It is the design.

The Leadership Insight

Leaders often assume faithfulness will be sustained by resolve. It won't. Long-term leadership exposes a different truth: what is not replenished will be depleted. What is not practiced will erode. What is not returned to God will slowly become self-reliant.

Stage 5 leadership recognizes that endurance is not achieved through intensity, discipline, or experience alone.

It is sustained through rhythm.

Manna teaches leaders to trust God for today.
Sabbath teaches leaders to stop striving.
Prayer teaches leaders to return to listen, confess, realign, and receive.

Growth happens through daily dependence *so that* leadership remains rooted in God rather than carried by habit, success, or stamina.

The Sustained Dependence Framework

Rhythms that protect faithfulness over time.

Receive Daily - Resist the Urge to Stockpile
Manna cannot be hoarded. Leaders must resist living on past encounters, past obedience, or past faithfulness.

Today requires today's dependence.

Honor Rest - Stop to Acknowledge God's Provision
Sabbath interrupts self-sufficiency. Leaders who rest declare that God sustains the work, not them.

Rest restores perspective.

Return in Prayer - Recenter Continually
Prayer is not an emergency measure. It is daily realignment. Leaders return to God to hear truth again and again.

Returning sustains clarity.

Repeat Faithfully - Trust the Power of Rhythm
Faithfulness is formed through repetition. Leaders who endure do not wait for motivation, they practice dependence consistently.

Rhythm builds resilience.

What This Looks Like at Work

In leadership today, dependence is often replaced by pace.

In corporate environments, leaders run on dashboards, metrics, KPIs, outcomes, and constant availability. In ministry or education, leaders carry emotional and spiritual weight without pause. In trades or operations, leaders push through fatigue, believing rest is optional.

But leaders who abandon rhythm eventually confuse endurance with exhaustion.

Dependence slows leaders down *so that* faithfulness lasts.

Reflection

- Where have you been relying on yesterday's manna?
- What rhythms currently support your dependence on God?
- Where might rest or prayer have become optional rather than essential?

Scripture to Read

"Give us this day our daily bread."
-Matthew 6:11 (ESV)

As you reflect on this verse, what does daily dependence look like in your current season?

Invite God Into This

Ask God to draw you back into daily dependence.

Invite the Holy Spirit to reestablish rhythms of rest, trust, and prayer. Pray for humility to receive what God provides today without clinging to yesterday.

Faithfulness is renewed daily.

Take the Next Step

- **Form a habit:** Begin or end each day acknowledging dependence on God.
- **Have a conversation:** Talk with someone about rhythms that sustain faithfulness.
- **Choose a new response:** Protect one rhythm of rest or prayer without apology.

Leaders do not finish well by pushing harder.

They finish well by returning, again and again, to the God who sustains them.

Keep Walking Worthy. Keep Pressing On

There is no finish line, only faithfulness

Leadership has a way of convincing us that the hardest part is getting started.

Learning the skills.
Finding our voice.
Stepping into responsibility.

But over time, most leaders discover a different truth. The greater challenge is not starting well. It is **continuing faithfully**.

Scripture never frames leadership as something we finish and move beyond. It frames it as a walk. A walk that unfolds across seasons, responsibilities, successes, failures, and quiet obedience.

Paul's words return us to where this journey began:

"I therefore, a prisoner for the Lord, urge you to walk in a manner worthy of the calling to which you have been called."
-Ephesians 4:1 (ESV)

Walking worthy is not about striving to deserve the calling. It is about living in alignment with a calling already received. It is about congruence between what we believe and how we lead, between faith and formation, between conviction and conduct. And yet, the walk is not passive.

Paul also reminds us:

"I press on toward the goal for the prize of the upward call of God in Christ Jesus."
-Philippians 3:14 (ESV)

Leadership requires movement.

We press on not because we have mastered the journey, but because obedience continues to call us forward. We press on when leadership stretches us beyond what once worked. We press on when the road gets long and the cost becomes familiar.

This is the tension leaders are invited to hold.

To **walk worthy** with integrity, humility, and attentiveness to God's forming work and to **press on** with endurance, perseverance, and trust that God is still at work ahead of us.

Throughout these pages, you have seen leadership form in stages not as a ladder to climb, but as a life to steward.

- Leadership begins internally, long before influence becomes visible.
- Leading others requires presence, trust, and courage.
- Release control as leadership multiplies beyond you.
- Cultures and systems speak even when you are not in the room.
- Daily dependence, discernment, and integrity over time.

Each stage asked something different of you. Each stage required you to let go of what once served you well and revealed that growth often comes through discomfort *so that* something deeper can be formed.

There is no stage where formation stops. There is no season where faithfulness becomes automatic. Leadership does not drift all at once. It drifts quietly when pace replaces prayer, when familiarity dulls discernment, when success becomes a substitute for obedience.

Leadership does not finish well by accident. It finishes well through small, repeated acts of faithfulness through returning, re-centering, releasing, and trusting God again and again.

This is not about perfection. It is about attention.

- Noticing when your walk becomes hurried.
- Recognizing when your pressing on turns into striving.
- Choosing obedience when no one is watching and humility when influence increases.

You will not always walk confidently. Some days the step will feel uncertain, costly, or slow. Take it anyway. Faithfulness is not measured by speed. It is measured by alignment over time.

So keep walking. Keep pressing on.

Not to prove yourself or earn the calling, but because the calling is still ahead of you. There is no finish line for leadership this side of seeing Jesus face to face. There is only the next faithful step.

And that is enough.

To the Leader Who is Curious, An Invitation.

If you have read *Walk Worthy. Press On.* and you are not entirely sure where you stand with Jesus, this page is for you.

You may not have picked up this book looking for a faith conversation. You may have been drawn to leadership, growth, or the desire to finish well. And yet, somewhere along the way, something resonated. You found yourself nodding, challenged, curious, maybe even unsettled in a good way.

Now that you have reached the end, I want you to know this clearly: there has never been pressure here.

Why Faith Comes Before Leadership

Every leader follows something, whether it is a vision, belief system or a definition of success. It can be a feeling or voice that shapes decisions when no one else is watching.

Throughout this book, you have seen that leadership flows from who we are becoming. At its foundation is a simple conviction: leadership ultimately flows from Who we are following.

Scripture tells us that we were created for relationship with God, to walk with Him, know Him, and live in community with Him (Genesis 1–2). Leadership was never meant to be independent. It was always meant to be rooted.

But Scripture is also honest about the fracture.

“For all have sinned and fall short of the glory of God.” (Romans 3:23, ESV)

Sin is not just about bad behavior. It is about separation. It is the posture of living apart from God’s leadership, choosing, subtly or intentionally, to lead our lives on our own terms.

And here is the reality every human leader eventually encounters: no amount of effort, discipline, wisdom, or success can bridge that gap.

God is holy, completely good, completely just, and nothing imperfect can earn its way back into His presence.

That is the problem we all share.

God Made the First Move

The Christian faith does not begin with striving. It begins with grace. From the very beginning, God made a way for relationship not through performance or perfection, but through a person.

“But God shows his love for us in that while we were still sinners, Christ died for us.” (Romans 5:8, ESV)

Jesus Christ is not simply a moral teacher or leadership example though He is the greatest leader who ever lived. He is the Son of God. Fully divine. Fully human. He lived the life we could not live, He died the death we could not escape and He did it once and for all.

“He himself bore our sins in his body on the tree, that we might die to sin and live to righteousness.” (1 Peter 2:24, ESV)

There is nothing to earn. Nothing to prove. Nothing to add. Salvation is not a reward. It is a gift.

“For by grace you have been saved through faith. And this is not your own doing; it is the gift of God.” (Ephesians 2:8–9, ESV)

What It Means to Follow Christ

Following Christ is not about becoming perfect. It is about relinquishing control. It is the decision to acknowledge that you cannot save yourself, to release the authority you have been holding over your own life, and to trust Jesus as Lord, not just advisor.

Scripture says it this way:

“If you confess with your mouth that Jesus is Lord and believe in your heart that God raised him from the dead, you will be saved.” (Romans 10:9, ESV)

That word Lord matters. It means leader. King. Authority.

The moment you stop striving and receive this free gift, you become a child of the one true King. From that moment on, your leadership journey changes, not because everything becomes easy, but because you are no longer leading alone.

Just like leadership, faith is a journey. The Bible calls this sanctification. It's the lifelong process of learning, growing, surrendering, and being shaped.

If questions come (and they likely will!) , I encourage you to talk with someone you trust: a pastor, a believing friend, or someone who can walk with you. Faith was never meant to be lived in isolation.

When You Are Ready

At some point, if you find yourself ready, ready to stop striving, ready to surrender control, and ready to follow rather than lead alone, you can pray. The prayer below is simply a guide, these specific words aren't a formula, they are words to help guide your willing heart.

God,
I come to You acknowledging that I do not have this all figured out. I have tried to lead my life on my own terms, and I recognize that I fall short.

I believe that You created me for relationship with You. I believe that Jesus Christ is Your Son, that He lived a perfect life, and that He died for my sins so that I could be forgiven and made new.

I lay down my need for control. I release the authority I have been holding over my own life. I receive the free gift of grace You offer, not because I earned it, but because You are merciful and good.

Jesus, I acknowledge You as Lord. Teach me how to follow. Shape my heart, my character, and my leadership as I learn to walk with You.

I trust You with who I am and who I am becoming.

Amen.

About the Author

Rachel Fiorentino believes leadership excellence is not something we arrive at, it is something we walk out, faithfully and intentionally, over time.

She is a Certified Professional in Talent Development (CPTD) with over 15 years of experience in adult learning and development, instructional design, and change leadership. Her work sits at the intersection of faith, leadership formation, and everyday life, helping leaders grow, lead, and finish well in the spaces where their influence matters most.

Rachel's journey has unfolded across many seasons, from homeschooling and ministry leadership to corporate learning and organizational transformation. Each chapter has reinforced the same conviction: leadership is not defined by title or momentum, but by faithfulness, especially when the work is unseen, the path is unclear, or the season feels long.

In her professional work, Rachel partners with organizations and leaders to translate vision into practice. She builds practical, human-centered frameworks that help teams navigate change, strengthen culture, and lead forward with clarity and conviction.

Her approach is grounded, actionable, and deeply shaped by the belief that formation matters as much as outcomes.

Rachel is also a speaker, leadership coach, and author, known for weaving biblical truth with modern leadership insight in a way that feels honest, relevant, and usable. Whether working with executive teams, emerging leaders, or faith communities, she consistently calls leaders to show up with character, steward their influence well, and keep walking, one faithful step at a time.

Rachel lives in Arizona with her husband, Joe. They enjoy traveling, collecting Harley-Davidson chips along the way, and spending time with their four adult children and their growing families.

Life Skills Unlocked Series:

- Foundations for Success (Ages 10–12)
- Navigating New Challenges (Ages 13–15)
- Preparing for Independence (Ages 16–18)

motivateleadinspire.com ✦ rachel@motivateleadinspire.com

Motivate • Lead • Inspire is more than a brand name, it is a leadership philosophy. Founded by Rachel Fiorentino, this platform exists to equip individuals and organizations to grow from the inside out.

The heart represents motive, why we lead and who we are becoming.

The shoe represents movement, leadership is not passive; it requires action, courage, and forward motion.

The seedling represents legacy, what we plant through our influence will grow long after we are gone.

Through writing, speaking, consulting, and leadership development experiences, Motivate • Lead • Inspire challenges leaders to pursue growth with courage, lead with clarity and conviction, and finish well with both impact and integrity.

www.ingramcontent.com/pod-product-compliance
Lightning Source LLC
LaVergne TN
LVHW020706110826
845149LV00012B/2134

* 9 7 9 8 9 9 1 4 7 6 3 4 8 *